The Wrens 1917-77

A history of the Women's Royal Naval Service

Ushason

Also published by Educational Explorers

SERVICE WOMEN: WRNS, WRAC & WRAF
by Chief Officer Vivienne Reynolds, Major Elizabeth Saxon
and Wing Commander Helen Renton

in the MY LIFE & MY WORK series
edited by Rachel Bleackley

The Wrens 1917-77
a history of the
Women's Royal Naval Service

by Ursula Stuart Mason

with a foreword by
HRH The Prince Philip, Duke of Edinburgh, KG, KT.

 EDUCATIONAL EXPLORERS · READING

First published 1977
© *Stuart Mason Limited*

ISBN 0 85225 774 0 *casebound*
ISBN 0 85225 901 8 *limp edition*

British Library CIP Data

Mason, Ursula Stuart
The Wrens 1917-77
1. Great Britain. Royal Navy. Women's Royal
Naval Service — History
1. Title
359.3'48'0941 VA465.W/
Bibl.-Index

Published by Educational Explorers Limited
40 Silver Street, Reading, England
Set in 11pt Baskerville and printed in Great Britain by
A. Wheaton and Company, Limited of Exeter

CONTENTS

ILLUSTRATIONS

These are grouped in sections chronologically

Inset at pages 65 to 96

ACKNOWLEDGEMENTS

MY THANKS ARE DUE to so many people for their help, advice, encouragement and kindness. I am particularly grateful to HRH The Prince Philip, Duke of Edinburgh, KG, KT, for writing the foreword.
Thanks are due also to:

Admiral Sir David Williams, Miss S. V. A. McBride, Miss Mary Talbot, Dame Jocelyn Woollcombe, Dame Nancy Robertson, Dame Elizabeth Hoyer Millar, Dame Jean Davies, Dame Margaret Drummond, Dame Marion Kettlewell, Miss Daphne Blundell, the Dowager Marchioness of Cholmondeley, Miss Joan Carpenter, the families of the late Dame Katharine Furse and Dame Vera Laughton Mathews; the Keeper, Public Record Office, and his staff, especially Mr. N. Evans; the Director, National Maritime Museum and his staff, especially Mr. A. W. H. Pearsall, Mr. J. Munday, Dr. R. J. B. Knight, Mrs A. M. Shirley, Mrs E. Wiggans, Miss D. Osbon, Mrs M. Patrick, Mr. B. Tremain, Mr. L. Walker, Miss P. Blackett, Mr. Porter and Mr. Beatty; Superintendent K. Morgan, Superintendent M. Sherriff, First Officer A. Savill, First Officer P. Williams, Second Officer V. Hattersley, Second Officer M. M. James, Second Officer E. Patrick; Rear Admiral P. W. Brock, Rear Admiral E. F. Gueritz, Mr. J. W. H. Bolton, S/Ldr. J. D. Braithwaite, Lt. W. G. Bruty, the Rev. C. P. de Candole, Cdr. R. Compton-Hall (Submarine Museum), Lt. Cdr. A. R. Davis, Mr. G. N. Johnstone, Cdr. B. S. Mallory, Maj. A. E. Marsh, Maj N. P. McLeod, Cdr. J. H. Middleton, Capt. J. S. Mitcalfe, Cdr. S. A. B. Morant, Mr. Noon, Lt. Cdr. H. S. Palmer, Lt. Cdr. E. V. Quickenden, Capt. G. H. Roberts, Mr. R. Taylor, Mr. R. C. Tetley, Group Capt. E. L. Tomkinson, Mr. P. Wilson, Lt. Cdr. R. Perfitt, Lt. Cdr. D. White, Mrs. U. Bowyer, Maj. A. J. Donald (RM Museum), Miss K. M. Foley, Miss E. F. Jossaume, Mrs. F. Lewis, Mrs. Francis, Mr. S. Pollard, Miss J. Preston, Miss W. Pringle, Mrs. B. Rolls, Mr. R. L. Pennells (Royal British Legion), Mr. A. K. Boyle, Mrs. Sheila Miller, Lt. Cdr. A. M. Pinsent and the Ladies Naval Luncheon Club, Mrs. D. W. Bazalgette and the Queen Anne Club, Mr. Keith North; Capt. A. G. Ellis, USN, Mrs T. B. A. Glazener-Hamers (MARVA); Chief Wren Nauta (MARVA), Cdr. Z. Ringvold, RNN, Cdr. G. Vido (DWNC), Vice Admiral H. Frohlic (PFAM), Miss E. Hill (WRANS), Mrs Harvey Stubbs (WRCNS); Mr. F. H. Lake (MOD library); Mr. George Naish; Mrs. M. Greenway, Mrs. P. Jenkin, Miss F. Mason, Mrs. M. Currie and the Association of Wrens, Mrs. E. Goudge and Miss K. Kevis (WRNS Benevolent Trust). Miss J. Frame (WRNR) and members of the WRNR Association (London); Mr. W. Wilkinson (Navy News).

1917–1919: Lady Ashton, Mrs. E. A. Ball, E. G. Barnes, Mrs. L. Barrett, Mrs. B. Browne, Miss H. Buckmaster, Mrs. M. Christian, Mrs. W. Drudge, Miss O. Franklin, Mrs. V. M. Frater, Mrs. M. Fuchs, Miss W. M. Glew, Mrs. M. Holroyd, Mrs. I. N. Horsey, Mrs M. Inggs, Miss G. D. Jackson, Mr. E. J. Kelly, Mrs. Q. M. Lowe, Mrs. M. McGegan, Mrs L. Newbery, the late Mrs. L. Paton, Mrs. R. A. E. Prescott, Mrs. N. Pyett, Miss E. Roberts, Mrs. J. A. Rossiter, Mrs. M. Strange, Mrs. D. E. Stoate, Miss C. M. Stewart-Tough, Mrs. I. M. Vaughan, Mrs. R. Walters.

1939–45: Mrs. M. Anderson, Miss C. Avent, Mrs. J. Baker, Mrs. L. G. Barlee, Miss M. E. Barralet, Miss M. Baugh, Mrs. A. Bell, Mrs. J. Birchard, Mrs. O. Bird, Mrs. M. A. Bleach,

Miss N. W. Boyle, Mrs. B. Bridge, Miss J. Bridgland, Lady Brind, Mrs. B. Browne, Mrs. R. Bryant, Miss H. Buckmaster, Mrs. M. de Burgh-Percival, Mrs. M. T. Caffrey, Mrs. N. Connolly-Batisti, Miss M. A. Cooper, Mrs. E. M. O. Crane, Mrs. Crisp, Mrs. J. Dallyn, Mrs. A. Dawe, Mrs. P. M. Drake, Mrs. V. Edwards, Mrs. J. Fisher, Miss G. L. Forfar, Mrs. H. S. T. Fletcher, Mrs. J. Franklin, Miss J. Frame, Mrs. M. Friendship, Mrs. B. M. Fussell, Mrs. B. Greenhalgh, Mrs. B. Gibbons, Miss M. N. Hailey, Mrs. P. A. Harding, Miss D. E. Hardy, Mrs. M. Harris, Mrs U. Hay, Mrs. M. Heigham, Miss S. M. Henderson, Mrs. K. Hill, Miss P. Hoare, Mrs. C. A. Hounsell, Mrs. I. N. Horsey, Mrs. F. Hugill, Mrs. K. Hull, Mrs. P. Inverarity, Mrs. C. Jarrett, Mrs. B. Johnston, Mrs. J. L. B. Joly, Miss N. K. Kellard, Mrs. M. Larson, Mrs. J. Laughton, Mrs. E. Lawson, Miss S. W. Lawson, Miss L. Leete-Hodge, Mrs. M. P. Lewis, Mrs. R. Lilley, Miss P. M. Lloyd, Miss M. Luckham, Mrs. J. Maclennan, Mrs. N. A. Marsh, Mrs. M. Marshall, Mrs. J. Marston, Mrs. H. M. Martin, Mrs. S. Martin, Mrs. A. Masters, Mrs. V. Mills, Mrs. M. L. Morris, Miss P. Neale, Miss P. K. Neale, Mrs. E. M. Nelson-Ward, Mrs. J. Nettleton, Mrs. J. M. E. Newman, the Misses Nichols, Mrs M. Perriam, Mrs. M. Penson, Dr. M. E. Plumb, Mrs. E. Prentice, Mrs. H. Rance, Mrs. K. E. Reaney, Miss G. Riley, Mrs. O. M. Rossiter, Mrs. J. A. Rossiter, Mrs. S. A. Russell, Mrs. P. Rutherford, Mrs. V. Selwood, Mrs. J. Shead, Mrs. O. Shelton, Mrs. M. Shepherd, Mrs. R. Shrago, Mrs. M. Stevens, Mrs M. Stickland, Mrs. M. Still, Miss J. C. Sutton, Mrs. M. Thompson, Mrs. N. Thompson, Mrs. M. R. Thorne, Mrs. R. Tiddy, Mrs. D. S. Timmermans, Mrs. N. Torbell, Miss P. Viola, Miss M. Warner, Mrs. J. Wheale, Mrs. G. L. Whiteley, Mrs. M. Williams, Mrs. Wingate, Mrs. O. Wrathall, Mrs. R. Rigg (WRCNS).

Post-1945: Mrs S. Berrecloth, Mrs. J. Blanchard, Mrs. P. A. Buckley, Mrs. P. J. Ford, Miss D. Foreman, Mrs. R. Short, Miss K. Strudwick, Mrs. B. Wilson.

The Imperial War Museum for permission to use five of their photographs. The Bodley Head for permission to quote from *Blue Tapestry* by Dame Vera Laughton Mathews (Hollis & Carter). The Keeper, Public Record Office, for permission to quote Sir Eric Geddes' letter to King George V (ADM 1/8506/264 Crown copyright). The Director WRNS for access to and use of Dame Katharine Furse's papers and WRNS archives (the *Dauntless* papers), now on loan to the National Maritime Museum.

USM

BUCKINGHAM PALACE.

     I am delighted that normal feminine reluctance to admit the passing of the years has been overcome in this welcome history of the first 60 years of the Women's Royal Naval Service. It is strange to think that it was only a short time after the suffragette campaigns for the emancipation of women that the Service was founded and that almost immediately the members found themselves doing things which would have been unthinkable a few years earlier.

     In the 1939 war numbers increased to 5,061 officers and 69,574 ratings and the range of tasks undertaken grew wider still. The Service is smaller again now, down to 250 officers and 3,000 ratings, but it is a wholly integrated and very welcome part of the Royal Navy.

     I suppose there will always be well-meaning people who will question the idea of women becoming directly involved in the unpleasant business of war through membership of the Services. To those men who make their careers in the Services it is not warfare as such which exercises their minds, but the wish to protect and defend their homeland and their fellow citizens. The fact that women are prepared to help them in this is strangely comforting and encouraging and I can assure all readers that the men of the Royal Navy, past and present, have the highest respect, affection and regard for the girls who serve in the W.R.N.S.

     Wrens are the Royal Navy's special breed of bird and we all offer them our best wishes on their Diamond Jubilee.

1977.

*My special thanks are due to Charles Miller
for his patience, help and constructive
criticisms and suggestions*

USM

INTRODUCTION

WHEN I AGREED TO WRITE the script for an exhibition to mark sixty years of the Women's Royal Naval Service, the then Director (Miss Mary Talbot, CB) said she hoped that the considerable research needed and all the resulting material would not be lost, but might perhaps be published in book form.

At the time I thought the script would be completed first and the book would follow, but as it happens this has been reversed.

I asked serving and former members of the Service to share their memories with me — increasingly recognised as a most valuable source of social history, but often underestimated — and at once got 200 replies to one letter in one newspaper.

While many of these recollections and others have been used, it has not been possible to include them all, nor to mention every category and unit, nor every outstanding officer or rating, not even every act of bravery or devotion beyond the call of duty.

I am sorry, but it is solely because of space limits.

Recollections, however interesting, are only part of a history. I have consulted original sources (such as Dame Katharine Furse's papers from 1917-1920) and have been able to read and quote from many other papers and letters not used — or sometimes even seen — before. I have talked to many who have been Wrens at some time or another, or who have had them on their staff or served with them.

There has been some two years of patient 'digging' to get the facts right and check people's memories against the records.

In the process I have learnt much about the Service and the women who have shaped it. It has left me more proud than ever to have been one of them.

URSULA STUART MASON

1

BIRTH OF THE SERVICE

MOST PEOPLE THINK that the Women's Royal Naval Service began in 1939. In fact it started in November 1917 and its birth certificate is, to all intents and purposes, a letter from the then First Lord of the Admiralty to the then Sovereign, King George V, a professional Naval officer, dated 26 November 1917:

'Sir Eric Geddes, with his humble duty, begs to inform Your Majesty that the Board of Admiralty have under consideration the possibility of substituting women for men on certain work on shore directly connected with the Royal Navy, and as a result of full enquiry, it is recommended that a separate Women's Service should be instituted for the purpose.

'It is submitted for Your Majesty's approval that the Service should be called THE WOMEN'S ROYAL NAVAL SERVICE, and that the members of this Service should wear a distinctive uniform, details of which will be submitted to Your Majesty for approval in due course.

'The Service would be confined to women employed on definite duties connected with the Royal Navy and would not include those serving in the Admiralty Departments or the Royal Dockyards or other civil establishments under the Admiralty.

'At the request of the Board, Dame Katherine Furze (*his spelling*), GBE, has accepted the position of Director of this Service, and she will be responsible under the Second Sea Lord for its administration and organisation, including the control of the members when off duty, and the care of their general welfare.

'It is humbly submitted that Your Majesty may be pleased to express your approval of these proposals.'

13

Rubber-stamped in red on this is 'The King has signified his approval', initialled EHB in pencil, dated 28 November 1917.

On the same day Sir Oswyn Murray, Secretary of the Admiralty, minuted to the First Lord: 'The King has now signified his approval and the notice is being issued to the Press. The Fleet Order and Office Memorandum may therefore also be issued.'

It had all been done with speed in the event, although the original idea had been mentioned as early as April.

On St George's Day Lady Rocksavage (later the Marchioness of Cholmondeley) had invited Sir Eric Geddes to drinks. He was desperately worried about the deteriorating manpower situation in the Navy.

She said she turned to him: 'Why don't you use women for shore jobs such as driving and typing? The Army does — why not the Navy?'

Sir Eric 'looked stunned. I don't think it had occurred to him before.'

Already women were doing men's work in factories and dockyards, and the Women's Auxiliary Army Corps was providing 'female substitution' to relieve soldiers for fighting duties.

Sir Eric had asked if the Navy could share the WAAC but no decision had been reached. By the autumn he decided the Navy must move on its own, set up its own women's corps, and he sought the best possible leadership for it.

It was common knowledge that Dame Katharine Furse, who had gained her GBE for her Red Cross work, was about to resign, because of irreconcilable differences, and that many on the staff at Red Cross headquarters in London would be resigning with her.

One of her friends and colleagues on committees was Mrs J. Chalmers Watson, Controller of the WAAC, and a doctor's wife from Edinburgh, who was also Sir Eric's sister.

On November 11 she telephoned Dame Katharine at her brother's request. She was invited to lunch at his house, 30 Queen Anne's Gate, at one o'clock that day (a Sunday). Dame Katharine's note of this call read: 'She told me he wished me to take on a Naval organisation of women.'

Sir Eric was blunt. 'He thought the best cure (for the War Office's tardiness) would be a "bomb shell" from the Navy. He was going to tell the Adjutant General he could not wait any longer and intended immediately setting up a competitive organisation of women for service with the Navy.'

Dame Katharine thought competing organisations wrong: co-ordinating women's groups to work with the Government would be better. Another Geddes, Sir Auckland, was Minister of National Service, and wanted to 'get powers' to do this and 'to insist upon all recruiting being done through National Service.' She added: 'If we started now we could later be brought under the bigger scheme.

'I told Sir Eric and Mrs Chalmers Watson that I must leave myself in their hands as I was only anxious to help where I could help most.'

Sir Eric promised to see the Second Sea Lord who would get in touch with Dame Katharine: 'I liked Sir Eric tremendously and felt that he was really powerful and would get good work out of one.'

In her autobiography (*Hearts and Pomegranates* published in 1940) she wrote of her first interview:

'I saw Vice Admiral Sir Herbert Heath, the Second Sea Lord at the Admiralty, on the 12th, finding Rear Admiral M. Culme-Seymour, Director of Mobilisation, and Sir Oswyn Murray, as well as an officer of the RN Air Service, with a scheme for the use of women in air stations.

'Sir Herbert outlined the Admiralty proposals, telling me I should be a "director" which was a Naval term, we discussed details relating to terms of service for women, and I was asked to "put in a scheme".

'Before leaving I asked for a book to help me to learn Naval organisation, of which I was ignorant, though I had just managed to learn something about the Army. My question evoked great puzzlement, but a messenger was sent to fetch a Navy List, which they handed me solemnly.

'Knowing the book . . . in my midshipman stage as a child, I realised it would not be much help at this juncture, when my need was to learn Naval organisation, terms, customs, traditions, etc. to say nothing of regulations.

'Walking up Waterloo Place afterwards I went into Hugh Rees's book shop which produced *King's Regulations for the Navy* and this solved my difficulty and became our "bible" for the WRNS.'

While she was in a book shop the Second Sea Lord was at a committee where it was decided to approve the formation of a Naval unit on the lines of the WAAC. He was asked to make the necessary

arrangements for establishing the Service, and arranging accommodation for its Headquarters staff.

Dame Katharine noted that no more than 10,000 women would be
required and these would be mainly cooks, clerks, writers, and
painters for trawlers:

> 'They did not propose to touch the dockyards but would want
> women for sail-making, wire netting, etc.
>
> 'They said there would probably be a good deal of opposition
> and told me that one of my duties would be to go round and see
> where women could be used as they thought one could probably
> find a lot more openings than were admitted by the officers in
> charge.
>
> 'They were extraordinarily nice . . . The pay officer who had
> been taking notes during the meeting ran after me afterwards
> and begged me to give him notes which he could write up as he
> had not been able to understand anything that was going on . . .'

She wrote to Sir Eric Geddes on November 13 that she had promised
to help.

> 'Having just learnt something of the Army I will do all I can to
> learn something of the Navy, but it is very like starting on a new
> language, and I may be slow to take it up. Thank you for giving
> me the chance.'

Sir Eric replied on November 14:

> 'No question of the advancement of the women's cause, or
> anything of that kind, affects me in the slightest . . . I and the
> Second Sea Lord are sure we shall benefit by your help, and I
> am quite sure you will find him anxious to help you in your task
> in every possible way.'

That day Dame Katharine formally resigned from the Red Cross.
Her criticisms of the living conditions for VADs attached to
temporary military hospitals had not been well received by her
superiors. She dealt, with great dignity, with letters published in *The
Times*, and consequent distasteful publicity, and spent the few days
between her Red Cross and WRNS appointments in planning the
latter.

On November 17 she left some questions for the Second Sea Lord.
Was it possible to have a pass to the Admiralty? What is a director? Is

the head of the women's organisation to have this rank and how does it compare with those with whom she will be working at the Admiralty?

May two or three of us decide upon what we consider to be a suitable uniform for the officers of the new organisation in order that we may get it immediately? May we adopt Naval buttons and badges or must this question wait for further discussion and approval?

In drawing up the scheme may we improve on WAAC conditions to ensure greater welfare for the women? When shall we be actually required to take up our duties? Will it be possible to have a car attached to our office?

Three women — Dame Katharine, Mrs Tilla Wallace and Miss Edith Crowdy — spent some days working on draft regulations. Dame Katharine went on her first visits to Naval establishments — the Royal Naval College, Greenwich, which had requested fifty waitresses, and the Crystal Palace where it was thought the first training centre might be set up. On November 23 she was appointed Director.

By now the agreed title for the Service was the Women's Royal Naval Service, and already people were referring to it as the Wrens.

Some of the other suggestions for a title make one shudder to think of the sailors' reactions: the WANKS or Women's Auxiliary Naval Corps; WNS or Women's Naval Service; WANS or Women's Auxiliary Naval Service; and RNWS or Royal Naval Women's Service. At first the Admiralty demurred at 'Royal' but later agreed to it.

Choice of uniform was important because what one wears is important for a woman. Certainly the first Director and those who helped her, designed well, for the basic officers' uniform of her day is still that of sixty years later, and has formed also the basis of the modern ratings' wear.

The Treasury forbade the WRNS to wear gold lace 'because of the wasting of gold' and this was accepted 'because gold lace is definitely the prerogative of the men'.

'So,' wrote Dame Katharine, 'we chose a royal blue lace and adopted the curl in the shape of a diamond, and the three-cornered velour hat we had tried to get for the VADs before the war.' It was edged in black Naval braid and bore a Naval badge embroidered in blue. Lady Cholmondeley vowed that they copied a hat she had bought in Paris and often wore.

Eventually Susan Barter, kitted up as a rating in a long, shapeless dress, tied in the middle, with a small version of a Naval rating's collar, pudding basin hat, thick black stockings and heavy footwear, and the Director in the officer's dark navy suit, white shirt, black tie, tricorne hat and leather gloves, went round to the Second Sea Lord for approval.

He took them to Sir Eric Geddes, who examined every detail. He pointed to the Director's buttons. 'She's got Admiral's buttons,' he said, 'why?' Admiral Heath explained that she was equivalent in rank to a Rear Admiral and therefore ought to wear the buttons with a laurel wreath round the anchor. Upon this they were approved. The Deputy Director, who ranked as a Commodore, also wore these buttons with great pride.

Many from the Red Cross joined the WRNS as opportunity arose, among them Mary Cane and Winifred Dakyns as Assistant Directors. Isobel Crowdy came with Edith, but Rachel, the third sister, stayed with the Red Cross. Ethel Royden who was to do much for ex-Wrens in later years, was also one of the first to join. Women doctors were on the staff — Dr Annie Forster to April 1918, then Dr D. C. Hare as medical director, and Dr Bell as assistant.

Lady Cholmondeley (who was still Lady Rocksavage at the time) was told a typist was needed. Although she had never touched a typewriter and had no office experience she agreed to help.

On November 29 the Admiralty issued Office Memorandum no. 245 announcing the setting-up of the WRNS, that accommodation had been provided in the Admiralty for the Director, and that recruiting for officers was under way.

Recruiting of all women who wanted to join the WRNS had to be through the local employment exchange (a deterrent to many) and there was a WRNS officer on the interview panel. Many of those who applied did not reach the standards set by the Service and were turned down, although they were eligible for other work.

Later on, when the WRNS had a recruiting drive, the Civil Service women representatives on the panels complained at the maintenance of these high standards and asked — in vain — for them to be lowered.

The first WRNS officers knew how important it was to establish the Service's reputation; compromise was not possible. Their insistence meant that maintenance of standards was a corner stone of the Service, and one which has continued to influence recruiting of all ranks and ratings to this day. The Navy can be thankful for this.

To understand why the setting of standards was so important one must try and understand the way in which our society was organised in 1917 — a completely different world from the one we live in.

It had been permissible for some years for some women to earn their living in office work, and for a considerably longer period women had been working in industry, often under appalling conditions as cheap labour, had been in domestic service, in nursing or engaged in 'cottage industries' — sweated labour — in their own homes.

It had not been considered 'quite the thing' for a middle class woman, however well educated, to earn her living at anything, although some had broken through and qualified as doctors against considerable opposition and there were some distinguished teachers. It was certainly *not* 'the thing' for an upper class or aristocratic woman to do so.

A good many women had been involved in the pre-1914 campaign to gain the vote. As soon as war broke out the Suffragettes publicly announced that all their energies would be devoted to winning the war — the Scottish Union of Suffrage Societies, for instance, changed themselves into the Scottish Women's Hospitals Organisation.

Women from 1914 on were able to find work in engineering, the public services, in factories, in munitions, and other occupations not normally designated as 'women's work'. They surprised men by 'their high pitch of excellence'.

By contrast a minority of women refused to change their way of life. An advertisement in 1916 was headed: *Buying this coat helped the Germans.*

The material had been shipped from abroad using space that should be set free for food and other necessary imports, its making-up had used skills which would be better used on war work, and the cost of it — £100 — would have been money better spent on munitions.

Women like Dame Katharine Furse who were fully engaged in war work were incensed by those who still spent a day shopping in town, gossiping, idling — not a day of leave from war service and a respite from hard work, not even a few hours spent away from a young family, but simply the unproductive (as it seemed in the light of war) way of life they had always pursued.

2

THE MIDWIVES — AND OTHERS

THERE WERE THREE MIDWIVES at the birth of the WRNS—Sir Eric Geddes, Sir Herbert Heath and Dame Katharine Furse.

Sir Eric was a strong personality with a lively business background who became Controller of the Navy in the spring of 1917, was elected M.P. for Cambridge in the July and in September became First Lord and a Privy Councillor. The rise was meteoric, the capability enormous and the efficiency staggering.

The Second Sea Lord, Vice Admiral Sir Herbert Heath, was fourteen years older than Sir Eric, and the son of an Admiral. He had commanded cruisers at the Battle of Jutland, been Admiral Superintendent of the Dockyard at Portsmouth, and was made KCB in 1917. Although he was the father of two daughters his background was hardly that of an ardent feminist.

The most important perhaps was Dame Katharine, another strong personality. She had a good brain and a clear mind, with a grasp of detail and was a good organiser. She was determined, she knew what was wanted, and went for it.

She was the fourth daughter of John Addington Symonds, the writer and poet, who had hoped for a son, so that she grew up as a boy until her teens, and she married Charles Wellington Furse, the painter, who shared her love of mountains and walking.

They had two sons, and when the younger was only a few days old, she was tragically widowed, Charles Furse dying after an illness through which she had nursed him.

The time came when her boys were older, and she joined the Red Cross, throwing herself into VAD training. Later she wrote: 'My experience taught me many lessons as we (in the WRNS) passed through the stage of having little sense of discipline and *esprit de corps*, I, for one, being a complete individualist, never having been a member of a team before.'

There was an element of masculinity in Dame Katharine's make-up but with it was a gentle femininity and a charm which not only made the women who worked under her her warmest admirers, but also enabled her to gain maximum co-operation from Naval officers and civil servants alike.

They were not all easily won over: one was heard to say 'There's a woman called Furse downstairs—get rid of her'.

She gained her DBE in June 1917 but had been reluctant to accept it, partly because she felt honours in war should go only to those who had earned them through bravery, and partly because she knew she could not continue in the Red Cross.

Her sons had no inhibitions. Peter, already a Midshipman, wrote 'Congrats old Bird !!!!!!!' while Paul, who was to become a Rear Admiral, wrote: 'Hereby I wish to convey my heartiest appreciation and congratulations of your being made a Dame'. Lizzie, the family cook, did not at all like the title 'because she often used the term "an old dame" in disparagement'.

Dame Katharine's own reactions were down-to-earth. 'When I give it in a shop I am often asked "Mrs or Miss?" What I like best is the use of the Christian name and few things are more irritating than being addressed as "Dame Furse" by people who would never think of saying "Sir Smith" to a man'.

In a short while it became GBE and she received the insignia—the collar (to be returned on her death), the investment badge and the star (to be retained by her relatives).

Her reaction to Sir Eric Geddes has already been noted, and of Sir Herbert Heath she wrote: 'He was our immediate senior and delightful to work with, being like a boy in the way he appeared to enjoy life, but taking full responsibility. He helped us in every way he could and always supported us when convinced that what we aimed at was right. He did not take this for granted, but when agreed he left the administration to us.'

The scheme for training of officers and women of the WRNS was a masterly document, especially when one realises that none of the women who drew it up had much experience of organising large numbers of people, or of business administration.

Quick and adequate training was necessary, they said, if the substitution of women for men was to be effective, and they recommended that during training women should live in hostels or camps.

'In addition to their technical training they will be learning discipline, general efficiency and smartness as well as becoming acquainted with the Standing Orders and Regulations of the Service.

'Many of the women who enrol in the WRNS may be unused to working with others and have but little realisation of the very real necessity for discretion and prompt obedience . . .'

It was considered essential for officers to be in a Receiving Depot hostel during their training:

'The success of the work of the WRNS will depend very largely on the finding and training of capable officers . . . The training course should be of at least two or three weeks duration, and enrolment should only be completed at the end of this period, when it is considered that the ladies who have been through the course are shown to be suitable in every way.

'The course should include lectures on the clerical work required, official correspondence, forms, indenting, returns, systems of accounts, etc.'

Naval officers lectured them at first (although the very first trained with WAAC officers and learnt mainly about Army Regulations) but later WRNS instructors took over.

An examination, said the scheme, should be held at the end of each course and on the results of this and a character assessment, candidates would be graded as Principals, Assistant Principals or Quarters Supervisors.

Chief Section Leaders and Section Leaders (or subordinate officers, known as CSLs and SLs) might be trained with the 'forewomen WAAC'. They learnt the theory of their category work, the use of forms, discipline, hygiene, management of women, drill, games and were to be 'imbued with the necessity for tact and courtesy when dealing with the women working under them, as well as with the men with whom they would be working.'

Those chiefly required were cooks, waitresses, laundresses, book-keepers, telegraphists, telephonists, wireless operators, motor drivers and other technical experts.

The training of drivers would be in two courses, a short one in mechanics for those who could already drive, and one of three weeks on driving and mechanics for those without previous experience.

Two courses were planned also for cooks. Two weeks for those with a knowledge of cookery, in the use of large quantities and the best use of rations, and one of a month for those without previous knowledge.

Laundresses would need seven to ten days training and this could be done while actually doing camp or hostel washing, while waitresses could also be trained 'on the job'.

> 'It should be made clear when the women are enrolled in the WRNS that those who fail to come up to the standard either in domestic or technical training will be required to serve in a lower grade than that for which they have been training.'

WRNS officers were to be selected by a board consisting of the Assistant Director WRNS Personnel, and not less than three WRNS officers, of whom the Director or Deputy Director would be one.

All women under training would have WRNS officers in charge of them, and these officers would work to the Assistant Director, WRNS Training.

The WRNS College was set up for officer training at Ashurst, near Crystal Palace, with Miss Thomson as principal. A new entry establishment for ratings, and a WRNS unit with stores ratings, writers, despatch riders, and drivers, were established at Crystal Palace, in South London. The officer in charge was Vera Laughton, a young journalist, and the daughter of Sir John Laughton, the Naval historian. She was to exercise a lasting influence on the Service.

3

GROWING PAINS

ON FEBRUARY 4, 1918, ADMIRALTY FLEET ORDER 414 *Women's Royal Naval Service — Arrangements* appeared, embodying much of the scheme.

Originally it had been thought that ratings would be immobile, living at home, in or near a port, but there was a need for mobile ratings and many volunteers from areas nowhere near a port had offered their services.

It was an early duty of newly appointed officers to find buildings suitable to accommodate mobile ratings — at Portsmouth, for instance, the Lion and Miller's Hotels were taken over.

Immobiles had to have a mess-room or similar accommodation near their work.

Mobile and immobile officers were accepted but Directors, Principals and Quarters Supervisors could only be selected from the former.

An earlier statement about not recruiting from women already employed in offices and dockyards by the Navy was ignored: 'Women engaged for Naval duties before the formation of the WRNS will be gradually absorbed into that Service.'

Pay was set. The Director got £500 per annum — and Dame Katharine said: 'I remember feeling so wealthy, when first appointed, that I promptly had lunch and half a bottle of Chianti at a restaurant near Victoria to celebrate the occasion. The sudden addition to one's income was very pleasant.'

The Deputy Director was paid £400, Assistant Directors £300, and Assistant Deputy Directors £250. Divisional Directors were paid £250, Deputies £200 and quarters.

Ratings got paid on a weekly basis. The highest rates were Superintending Section Leaders or Chief Section Leaders in a number of categories who got 45s a week. Unskilled categories were paid at a lower rate.

All mobile ratings got a gratuity, paid in arrears, at 13s a quarter. Learners in all categories were paid 25s or less.

Deductions were to be made from pay for absence without leave, or excess of paid leave ('being adrift') of one day's pay for each day's absence.

Immobiles living in their own homes would find their own board, lodging, service and washing. All members of the WRNS accommodated in hostels or lodgings would have a deduction at a fixed rate (15s 6d a week for officers, 14s a week for ratings) if their conditions of service did not include free board, lodging and washing.

Rations were allocated, and such matters as transfers, discharges, casualties, redress, leave and so on were dealt with in precise language.

So was travelling: 'Officers of the WRNS will travel first class, and women third class.' And 'the concession enabling a standard meal at a cost of 1s to be obtained at railway refreshment rooms applied to the WRNS.'

On enrolment forms was printed 'You are hereby warned that if, after enrolment, it is found that you have wilfully given a false answer to any of the questions, the Board of Admiralty or any person duly authorised by them retains the right to terminate any contract that they may have entered into with you.'

The first Headquarters was in a small office in Central Buildings, Westminster, but this rapidly became too small, and 15 Great Stanhope Street, a corner house, was taken. It opened on January 7, 1918.

Their Lordships approved the appointments of the Director, Deputy and two Assistant Directors on December 17, 1917, and officers' training having officially started on January 7 (1918) the next important date in WRNS history is January 18 when the first officers were appointed to bases and stations.

There were Divisional Directors in London, Portsmouth, Chatham, Devonport, Edinburgh and Cardiff, with Deputies at Immingham for the East Coast, and at Harwich. A Principal, acting Deputy Divisional Director, was at Liverpool.

By March 18 the number of ratings already on duty or reporting that week totalled about 850 in England and Wales, and about 200 in Scotland.

A Division was made up of twenty or more Sub-Divisions each under an officer called a Principal. A Sub-Division included two or more Companies under Principals or Deputy or Assistant Principals, and in some cases Sections under Chief Section Leaders (like modern Chief Wrens).

For instance, the London Division included the Depot; Crystal Palace Company; Officers' Training Hostel; Greenwich Company; Wormwood Scrubs (RNAS) Company; Admiralty Garage Company; Hotel Cecil (Air Board) Section; Deptford offices of HMS PRESIDENT Company.

Headquarters was headed by the Director, with the Deputy immediately below her. The Assistant Director Recruiting was Muriel Currey, who at a later date became responsible instead for Demobilisation.

The Assistant Director for Personnel was Mary Cane, the Assistant Director (Administration) was Winifred Dakyns and Isobel Crowdy was Assistant Director for Inspection and Training.

From the beginning everything connected with the Royal Naval Air Service was kept separate. The formation of the Royal Air Force (by merging the RNAS and the Royal Flying Corps) was already planned and from early in 1918 the Women's Royal Air Force (then Women's Auxiliary Air Force) had its own Director. It was officially constituted on May 1 (although it existed from April 1) and WRNS serving on RNAS stations in Britain were to be transferred, completing by July 1.

However the hand-over seems to have been delayed for WRNS Acquaint 144 of November 8 listed stations being transferred as late as October and November.

WRNS had been asked on joining if they would be prepared to transfer when the time came. Those who had agreed duly handed back their WRNS uniform and put on the new WAAF one. Those who wished to stay in the WRNS were moved at the earliest moment to a Naval establishment. The separate records were easily available to the new Service and the change-over seems to have gone smoothly.

One only has to read their letters, look at their photographs and talk to them to know that the first WRNS were a lively generation. They must have been quite difficult to weld into a cohesive unit wherever they were drafted. The task cannot have been made easier with so many living at home and treating the whole exercise as a kind of normal job which helped the war effort and meant wearing a uniform (which gave them a certain status).

Their motives for enlisting were frequently misunderstood. In a letter of February 11, 1918, the Director told the Second Sea Lord that there had been scandal in the WAAC with allegations of immorality and there had been bracketing of the Wrens with the WAACs. She wrote:

'It is desperately hard on the WRNS that we should be involved in the WAAC trouble . . . What seems to be the best preventitive of rumours in our own Service is to run it on very considerate, human lines.

'The War Office is apt to run things on rule of thumb lines and I don't believe this is possible where women are concerned . . . I am impressing on my officers the immense importance of winning the women's confidence by explaining the conditions to them . . . and that we shall care very seriously for their proper well-being.

'If we can secure a nucleus of good and serious women and if we can make them proud and content to wear our uniform, they and their friends and relations will put up the best barrage against slander which can be provided.

'Can you help us by issuing an order or appeal or something to all Naval officers asking them to talk to the men to get them all to realise that they must help and protect the women and their reputation?'

Admiral Sir Herbert Heath issued a letter to Commanding Officers on the 20th on 'the use of women' ending with:

'May I therefore ask you to use your personal influence in assisting all concerned in viewing this effort on the part of the women in the right light.

'That is to say, that they are endeavouring to help the country to the best of their ability and that they ask only to be treated with that courtesy and respect which their sex demands.'

In her autobiography Dame Katharine wrote that the WRNS had very few cases of pregnancy or VD.

'In the former we discharged the women on benevolent grounds, but saw them safely through the process of child-bearing.

'In the latter we ensured treatment for them but did not discharge as our Medical Directors and I agreed that we should do more to maintain a moral code by humane treatment than by punishment, and the response certainly justified this belief.'

4

AND OVERSEAS TOO

Occasionally the Director felt that she and the WRNS must be a source of irritation and annoyance to Naval personnel who knew the regulations and customs as the women could not yet do. Accordingly when the organisation was running well she wrote in the summer of 1918 a kind of open letter.

After apologising for 'troubling unconscionably' many busy people she thanked the various Departments who had helped in getting the Service launched.

'We only hope that by our ultimate efficiency we may prove that the WRNS are worthy of all the kindness and assistance which have been accorded to them.

'At any rate we can promise zeal and alacrity in the performance of any duty assigned to us.'

The Director was indefatigable. Every conversation and every visit was noted in her own writing — which gave the impression that her thoughts were racing ahead of her pen.

She went almost everywhere there were WRNS, she inspected accommodation and working conditions, ate the food prepared for them, enquired into their leisure activities and encouraged them to take physical exercise.

She fostered the spirit of friendly competition, she asked questions about supplies of uniform (as late as April 1918 women reporting for duty were asked to bring overalls and aprons to wear over their civilian clothes while working), and she talked in a friendly, personal way which the women of all rates and ranks remembered and appreciated.

At Christmas 1917 and again in 1918 she sent every member a small card. She also gave each one a printed card in a WRNS-crested envelope, bearing a message from her and Nelson's eve-of-Trafalgar prayer. There were also two exhortations: 'Remember, the Empire expects that every woman will do her duty' and 'Fear God, Honour the King.'

Each woman received a confidential card for her pocket book with the Director's guidance on how she should behave in 'the circumstances of Naval service', so that she maintained the standards required of her.

Those who received Dame Katharine's cards kept them, and to this day they are among their most treasured possessions.

The WRNS served not only at home but also, at the earliest possible moment, overseas. (The Government had passed legislation enabling mobile women to go overseas in the Services if they so wished.)

The Headquarters of the Mediterranean Division was set up in Malta with 14 mobile and 17 immobile ratings and 16 officers, the greater number working in the Naval Staff Offices.

The first unit abroad was in Gibraltar, and there was another in Genoa. A small party of officers set out before the war ended to look at possible bases in Egypt, where sub-divisions were planned for Ismailia, Alexandria and Port Said. However they had only got to Malta by the time of the Armistice so stayed on, doing cypher and accountant work.

Miss I. M. Jermyn, Divisional Director, wrote: 'Malta is an extremely gay place, and the members have seen a great deal of the Royal Navy, having had the most wonderful opportunities of going over interesting vessels of almost every kind, and of several countries.'

She added: 'The Gibraltar sub-division has the great advantage of being able to get into Spain for day trips, a delightful experience for the ordinary, stay-at-home girl. . . . Some of the officers and ratings have been to Tangier by torpedo-boat for a day's trip.'

A sub-division was almost in being at Bizerta, on the African coast, but the first party was recalled on its way out from England.

Had the war continued there would have been a large Division in the Mediterranean, Adriatic and Aegean, and there would have been WRNS at Corfu, Taranto, Naples, Syracuse, Marseilles and possibly Oran and Mudros.

Tropical uniform looked smart but as it was the adapted UK uniform it must have been very hot to wear. Officers' uniform was similar but in white, with white stockings and shoes, and wide solar topees.

Ratings wore the unpopular coat-frock in white with blue sailor collar, blue belt, white cover on the pudding basin hat, and white shoes and stockings.

CSLs and SLs wore a mixture: sometimes a dark jacket and long white skirt; sometimes a white jacket. Collars and ties were worn despite the heat. WRNS served in France and Belgium where the 'home' uniform was worn.

In Britain the WRNS were not only in the great ports but also in places like the remote RN Air Stations in Llangefni, Anglesey, and Walney Island.

They were, too, in scattered units far from the Navy — in North East England, in Cornwall and Devon. Eight ratings and an officer served in the Scillies where the latter 'acted as a kind of hostess to the base, keeping an eye on its manners, morals and socks.'

The substitution of women had begun in Plymouth in the Commander-in-Chief's office in September 1917, using civilians who were absorbed into the WRNS in March 1918. The largest number of WRNS was in the Royal Naval Barracks, the second largest in the Royal Marine Light Infantry Barracks.

Near the C-in-C's office and overlooking the Sound was the Signal Station 'a little turret containing RN pensioners on its upper deck and, below, the Naval Telephone Exchange where WRNS were first used in May 1918 to help the Chief Signal Boatswain. From August they had entire charge of both Exchange and message room, by day and night, under the Communications Officer.'

A company worked on board HMS APOLLO, depot ship for the 4th Destroyer Flotilla, as sailmakers, turners, fitters and clerks.

By October 1918 some 750 officers and ratings had been enrolled in the South Western Division.

The first (slightly reluctant) recruits in Portsmouth were drawn from women already working in offices and the dockyard, and the Division started on January 22, 1918.

First those with the RM Artillery at Eastney were enrolled, then units were quickly established at the RN Barracks, HMS EXCELLENT, HMS DOLPHIN, the Mining School, Paravane Department, Forton Barracks and the Signal School.

By November 1918 the Division totalled 1,148.

Scotland was no easy matter — from January 1918 right through to the summer senior Naval officers were 'nervous' of using women, fearing they might be indiscreet or not up to the job.

However the women who had joined had proved their worth by the autumn and the situation changed. Initially the Division's work was done in an Edinburgh hotel bedroom but after a month three rooms in Queen Street were taken over as offices.

At Inverness existing women staff were absorbed, and a large additional number recruited, while others at Granton, Oban, Ardrossan, Aberdeen and Peterhead were absorbed very quickly.

There were also WRNS at Rosyth and Grangemouth and by the Armistice 41 bases and offices were operational, with some 750 Wren ratings at work.

WRNS were to be found from the Orkneys and Shetlands in the far north to Luce Bay in the south, and from the Outer Hebrides to East Fortune. Stornaway, Leith, Lerwick and Glasgow all had units.

In addition some 50 officers were in charge of Admiralty mail offices and anti-gas depots, or working as de-coders, or signallers or as assistant paymasters.

There was difficulty in Liverpool in persuading those already working in the Naval offices to join. There was reluctance to accept discipline and authority, and a distaste for uniform. However as new WRNS were enrolled 'the others fell into line, attended the drills and soon formed a smart squad,' said the Divisional Director, Miss F. E. Warton.

Three weeks later, in April 1918, the first officers started work at the Holyhead base, and in May immobiles were at work at the RNAS, Walney Island.

The greater part of the WRNS duties in the Bristol Channel Division were clerical — on the Senior Naval Officer's staff, in bases, transport, DAMS and shipping intelligence offices.

That they could cope with heavy work-loads was demonstrated in a tribute from an officer, after his base closed. A Wren had been taken on as typist to an engineer officer. When the (male) civilian stores ledger clerk left she took on his whole-time job as well as her own.

She was in charge of the Engineer and Stores offices, kept all stores ledgers and accounts, and for weeks worked until 11 pm every night. Her officer was enormously impressed.

Miss M. James, who was in charge at Tynemouth, had an area which was temporary and so, after starting on March 20, 1918, was contemplating demobilisation by November 11.

The women were employed in small, scattered units with no more than 25 in any of them, and not many saw the Navy at work. Some in the signal room in the Senior Naval Officer's office managed to see the comings and goings of a great variety of ships on the Tyne. They were the lucky ones.

The East Coast Command was, in the words of Miss M. Isemonger (who became Humber Divisional Director) 'somewhat ahead of the Admiralty in regard to women's service.' From as early as November 1914 women were employed in the Naval offices at Hull and Grimsby, and others were taken on in the spring of 1917 at Immingham, where a Naval depot was built, and the Admiral made his headquarters.

WRNS worked in the signal station and the coding office, where, when the pressure was on, the same coders took 24 hours' continuous duty without failing.

The first women who ever learnt to adjust naval gyroscopes were taught in the torpedo shed at Immingham by an old Artificer. Others learnt to maintain and repair searchlight lamps and hydrophones; others to construct wire nets used against enemy submarines, to clean the mines attached to these nets, and the casings of depth charges. Some even undertook the priming of depth charges.

Harwich had two sub-divisions which never had their full complement of women for want of accommodation for them. At Shotley women cooked in the small galleys for men at the training establishment, but men had to cook for the boys because the women's quarters were never ready.

Cooks, telephonists and clerks had to live in the Pier Hotel, Harwich, and go on duty by boat. At Osea Island nearly all the domestic workers were women but if accommodation had been available there would have been boat-cleaners and other WRNS working in the engineering shops.

At Lowestoft the women cleaned boilers aboard trawlers and drifters, were sail-makers and did depth charge work. At Ipswich a small Naval telephone exchange was manned entirely by WRNS under a WRNS duty officer. At the anti-gas depot at Parkeston (closed in December 1918) Wrens repaired respirators brought to them from the ships.

Chatham Division also covered Dover, Deal, Sheerness, Broadstairs, Ramsgate, Hastings and Folkestone. Wren ratings worked in Chatham at the RN Barracks, the RM Barracks and with the RM Engineers. At the RN Barracks for instance 15 Wrens entirely replaced men on the day shift in the bakery, and made bread for 6,000 men.

WRNS in Dover acted as porters in the victualling stores, doing really heavy work such as loading vans with potatoes. Others worked on mine nets or gas masks (some officers went on board ships to give demonstrations on using the masks) and 18 were drivers and despatch riders at the Naval motor transport office. Others scrubbed life belts on the Admiralty Pier.

The Irish Division headquarters was at Kingstown, but the largest number of WRNS were employed at Larne, an important anti-submarine base. Substitution of women had been fully carried out there before the WRNS was formed.

All the women at Larne were immobile and 'when work was slack' they built a fine new landing stage. Their normal duties were those of clerks, messengers, storekeepers, net mineworkers, unloaders, on depth charges, hydrophones and so on.

The work in London has already been outlined, with its unique features of Headquarters and the central training establishment.

It was in London in June 1918 that King George V and Queen Mary celebrated their silver wedding and a Procession of Homage of the women's war organisations went to Buckingham Palace. Three thousand women marched through Hyde Park where Lieut.-General Sir Francis Lloyd took the salute.

The WRNS contingent drilled in Courtfield Gardens, Kensington, near the London Hostel, but local residents complained that they were ruining the gardens. However practising went on . . .

In the quadrangle of the Palace the King watched from a balcony as the women marched in and formed up, with the Queen and Princess Mary beside him.

When the parade was ready and at attention the Queen took her place on a canopied dais, where the King and Princess joined her. Miss Durham, Chief Woman Inspector, Women's Department, Ministry of Labour, presented an address, and the King spoke to the parade.

'No chapter in the history of this country's share in the war,' he said, 'will be more remarkable than that relating to the range and extent of women's participation.'

Afterwards the Second Sea Lord wrote to the Director:

'I must express to you my very sincere congratulations on the good appearance, deportment and smartness of the WRNS.

'I was very much struck by their general appearance of well-being and contentment.

'I hope you will let it be known to all concerned how proud we of the Navy felt of our WRNS.'

In November the Armistice was signed. The war 'to end all wars' was officially at an end. The primary reason for starting the WRNS no longer existed. The men who had been released for sea service — or those of them who survived — were to be brought home and would need shore jobs again.

But not quite yet.

5

'DEAD–BY ORDER OF THE BOARD'

THE DIRECTOR COULD NOT BEAR to lose the wonderful spirit which had been created in the WRNS – and neither could the women.

There had been those who had christened them 'the Prigs and Prudes' or 'the Perfect Ladies' and wished them otherwise. But in a very short time they had formed their own unique character.

It was this spirit and character which produced petitions for the retention of a permanent Service, signed by every woman in a unit; other women offered to serve without pay and in whatever way they could be useful to the Navy and the country.

There was a good deal of behind-the-scenes lobbying in high places – and in not so high, such as the London Hostel's pantomime. Written, produced and presented by themselves with a cast of 39, it was shown on New Year's Day 1919 in Kensington, and repeated in March when the Director was present, and the audience was almost exclusively a Service one.

One of the songs included the words: *K-K-Katharine, most wonderful Katharine, You're the only one for us in time of war; Should the c-c-call come in the f-future. We will rush to follow you once more.* The audience rose and gave her a great ovation.

Then over a thousand saw it at Chatham – among them Admiral Sir Doveton Sturdee – and more at Portsmouth and Greenwich.

But on February 19, 1919, the Admiralty Fleet Order went out announcing the gradual demobilisation of the WRNS 'as the requirements of the Service permit.'

The Order added:

'The Board desire to take this opportunity of placing on record their high appreciation of the work which this Corps has accomplished.

'The WRNS was brought into being at a time of great national emergency when it was necessary to release every man that could be spared for the active fighting forces.

'The rapidity with which the Corps was organised to that end and brought to a high state of efficiency constitutes a remarkable achievement and one that reflects the greatest possible credit on the Director and her officers and ratings.

'All who have come into contact with the WRNS have been impressed by their discipline, zeal and *esprit de corps* and the Royal Navy has felt justly proud of the Women's Service which the greatest war of all time called into being to work with us for the common end.

'This Order is to be brought by Commanding Officers to the notice of officers and ratings of the WRNS under their command.'

On May 2, 1919, there was a suggestion that Dame Katharine should report on the organisation of the WRNS with recommendations as to re-establishment if necessary. At once she wrote to Divisional Directors and others to ask for their advice and suggestions.

AFO 1753 issued on May 17, 1919, was the only WRNS Honours List of the war. It contained the list published in the London Gazette on May 9 — 49 officers and 22 ratings (together with Naval nursing sisters and VADs attached to WRNS units) 'brought to notice for valuable services in connection with the war.'

The Director and her Deputy were not mentioned. But three Assistant Directors — Mrs Cane, Mrs Dakyns (promoted from MBE) and Dr Hare — were made CBE (Mil). Divisional Directors and their Deputies and other officers were included, and ratings ranged from writers to an electrician, telephone operator to steward; two were drivers, one a mechanic and one a draughtswoman.

One Senior Writer, Dorothy French (now Stoate) received her BEM at a parade in Malta: 'I had to go smartly up to the Admiral presenting the medal, salute, wait for him to make a little speech, shake hands and give a smart salute at the end. Alas I forgot the salute and remembered only with my back to him . . . To this day I can hear the quiet groans of the Wrens.'

Chief Section Leader Mavis Carter (now Strange) got a handwritten letter, after being demobilised, from the Recruiting Officer in Birmingham (a Major, Royal Marines) inviting her to discuss whether she wanted her BEM presented publicly, or in his office with her friends and the recruiting staff present. She chose the latter but her father, an Army Major, thought she deserved better.

On July 19 the great Peace Parade marched in London, with a large contingent of very smart Wrens. Beforehand there were drill practices in Hyde Park at which Winsome Bull (later Kemp, who died while this was being written) was drill officer, exhorting everyone to do their best.

Dame Katharine wrote: 'I shall never forget Bull running beside me saying, with tears in her voice, "Oh, Ma'am, *do* try to look important".'

The day before, the Director and two others had walked the course—seven miles of it—to find out what was involved.

On the day a policeman at Stanhope Gate, as they passed, said 'Well done, Wrens' and at Sloane Street it could be the strain was showing for there was a call from the crowd 'Smile'.

They were perhaps most deeply moved by something that happened after they had passed the King, standing on his platform in front of Queen Victoria's Memorial outside Buckingham Palace. Near the Achilles statue at the Park corner stood the Navy's most senior officers, almost all Admirals. Spontaneously as the Wrens went by they clapped. It was an action recalled to this day by survivors of the march.

The crowds in Trafalgar Square were so dense that the Wrens had to go through singly rather than six abreast, re-forming under Admiralty Arch as they went into the Mall. When it was all over they found it had lasted five hours.

On July 23 the Second Sea Lord, now Vice Admiral Sir Montagu Browning, wrote officially: 'I desire from personal observations, to congratulate the Officers and Ratings of the WRNS who took part in the procession on July 19 upon their marching and appearance which was most creditable to their Corps. The WRNS had thoroughly earned the right to be represented on this historic occasion with the Royal Navy.'

Sir Herbert Heath, now Commander-in-Chief Rosyth, wrote: 'So many thanks for the photograph of my dear WRNS keeping up their looks and discipline to the last. I did get a glimpse of you at the start as you were passing the Achilles statue and shouted my good morning from among the Admirals there assembled . . . it is so sad to think of the demobilising of such a splendid force.'

On July 28 the Director wrote to Admiral Browning:

'We are all very unhappy at the thought of leaving the Navy and
I am constantly being appealed to by ranks and ratings WRNS
with a view to our maintaining some sort of Reserve on an
honorary basis.

'We fully realise the necessity for our demobilisation but I
would very much like to be able to make an announcement to
the effect that all ranks and ratings — other than those discharged
for misconduct or unsuitability — are invited to join an Honorary
Reserve for the period of three years.

'This would ensure that our uniform remained protected and
would provide for our being able to mobilise again supposing
our services were required.'

She added that she would like to discuss the attaching of the WRNS
Reserve to the RNVR, organising it on VAD lines and perhaps drawing recruits from organisations such as the Girl Guides.

This was a new idea. She had earlier suggested a Reserve which
would cost the Admiralty nothing (a shrewd observation) being a
diminishing force, for only those who had served would be eligible to
join, and there would be no attempt to recruit.

No member would be paid but they would meet regularly, wear
uniform, maintain drill and other standards, and be in all respects
ready to serve again if so required.

The Admiralty declined the offer.

On August 4, anniversary of the outbreak of war, there was a Sea
Services Commemoration on the River Thames, a procession of craft
headed by the King in his State Barge. He embarked at Customs
House Quay, and disembarked at Cadogan Pier where the WRNS
provided a guard of honour. The return procession was headed by
the Lord Mayor of London as Admiral of the Port of London.

Five senior officers from WRNS Headquarters, together with 15
other officers and 24 ratings, embarked at Limehouse Pier in motor
lighters and actually took part in the River procession. Another 100
ratings had special places on the riverside, and a good view.

It was a splendid affair: steam vessels, landing and picket boats,
rowing barges, lighters, a motor life-boat, an ambulance launch,
motor lighters and drifters, gigs, and some seventy lifeboats filled
with parties representing pilots, fishermen, Naval nurses, Sea Scouts,

and every possible sea and river service. The Royal Navy manned twelve 12-oared cutters and four picket boats.

Many went on to the water in a variety of craft to watch. Many more were on board ships in the docks or watching from bridges or banks.

But the WRNS ceased to exist, by order of Their Lordships, on October 1, 1919, and final demobilisation papers were dated September 30. It had reached a peak of 5,054 ratings and 438 officers.

Immobile ratings were to all intents and purposes civilians and, being paid weekly, received seven days notice.

Mobile women were eligible for 28 days leave on full pay and allowances. All ratings were entitled to retain their uniform with cap ribbons, collars, buttons and badges.

After their leave had expired it was not, however, to be worn complete, except on such occasions as might be specially authorised. Each woman received a certificate of service on leaving her unit.

All ratings were entitled to 'Out of Work Donation Policies'. Mobiles for HM Forces policies, and immobiles for civilian policies. This was the equivalent of unemployment benefit.

For many women the prospect ahead was bleak. Some returned happily to the bosom of their families. Others went off to start their own homes with newly demobilised husbands. Yet others had to find jobs — and for all the talk about women's emancipation this was difficult. Those jobs available were badly paid and without career prospects.

Some of the Headquarters staff stayed on for a few days after the end, to clear up, but were not paid.

In fact, one gets the impression from notes in files that the Admiralty found them uncomfortable company and wished them gone.

No one seems to have said it in so many words but on a file, opened in December 1919, there is something that is somehow indicative. Boldly written across the cover is *Dead. Scheme dropped by Board order.* There is an illegible signature and the date 15.8.22. It was a file on the possible reorganisation of the WRNS in peacetime.

6

BEHIND THE STATISTICS

BEHIND THE STATISTICS WERE THE WOMEN. From many different backgrounds, each made of her WRNS service something individual and to her unforgettable. Those who survive—a dwindling number inevitably—still have vivid recollections and cherished mementoes.

Some remember things they did not much like. Discipline and drill, for example, were unpopular with women unused to such things.

Queenie Bishop (now Lowe) remembers that Lady Patricia Ramsay (Princess Patricia) was going to visit Portsmouth, and this meant drill practice for the Wrens under a PT instructor. 'Not enjoyed,' she said, 'by any of us, who did not take kindly to marching.'

Marjorie McGegan was a decoder in the War Registry in Whitehall until 'embodied' in the WRNS, working in the same office but suddenly under discipline: 'We were very strictly guarded by a martinet and worked three watches. Officers' rooms were out of bounds and I was in the dog-house for ages after a very innocent party with RNVR officers in an empty room.'

She also remembers 'No food was provided on duty and if there was an air raid and one was delayed for hours, one just starved.' (Echoes of all those healthy young women with sturdy appetites whose memories have included feeling hungry between meals.)

Rose Edmunds (now Walters) was another. She was a steward and while on a training course at Portsmouth lived in a hostel in Hampshire Terrace, which meant a march from barracks to hostel after dinner. This took the girls along Stanley Road where Rose's mother lived.

'We used,' said Rose, 'to eat about six-thirty so I was hungry again by ten. My mother used to prepare sandwiches and hand them to me on the march and give me a good-night kiss. I was warned about this and one night the petty officer caught me breaking ranks. I was reported and got 10 days' confined to quarters.'

40

This lively lass recalls another incident: a party of Wrens, going from an air station to another establishment, were changing trains at Lewes (Sussex) in 1918. 'As we got off the train a lot of German prisoners were on the platform, and one of them stepped out and spat at me. So I got out of line and spat at him. For that I got another 10 days' confined to quarters.' She was clearly unrepentant.

Some remember aspects of their jobs. Louisa Day (now Barrett) was a member of the galley staff at the Royal Naval College, Greenwich: 'As I remember my chief occupation was making toast — an eye-scorching operation. We also drilled — sometimes in Greenwich Park but mostly in the Painted Hall with Nelson's relics housed at the top end.'

Dorothy French (Stoate) worked at Felixstowe for Commander Samson, who devised a scheme to fly a plane off a ship's deck, which would get near enough to Heligoland to destroy the Zeppelins which were bombing Britain.

The first time Commander Samson himself flew the plane it went into the sea and he and it had to be hauled up. Alterations were made and the first operational flight 'bagged' a Zeppelin.

Mavis Carter (Strange) went to Headquarters from the Red Cross, and was put in charge of the post room, which entailed many trips up and down stairs every day delivering signals and mail. She remembers that ratings had to have permits before they could go out with commissioned officers in uniform.

'I even needed one to go out with my own father. So I applied for as many as I could, putting down the names of all my relatives and friends, so that I might always have a permit available if anyone came home unexpectedly.'

Mary Batterbury (now Christian) joined the WRNS in Queenstown, Ireland, and lived with her brother, an assistant paymaster: 'I remember that when my brother and I left our flat together and walked about 50 yards before going our different ways to work, ten shillings was deducted from my pay as a fine for walking in public with an officer.'

Although the WRNS motto was *Never at Sea* some of them managed to take to the water — Gladys Wilburn (now Barnes) for one. She 'captained' a large motor launch, the BALMACAAN, which wore the White Ensign, and operated from Southwick and Shoreham Harbour, Sussex.

The work at 'Mystery Towers' was experimental and secret. Her launch had to tow a model about after dark and behind canvas screens while engineers experimented with it. 'But the war ended before it could be used.'

Jane Rossiter gave up her job as a civil servant early in 1918 to join her Army husband in Devonport. She sought a job in a Naval shore establishment, and became a writer in the office on board a training ship moored in the Hamoaze, made up of two linked vessels POWER-FUL and ANDROMEDA. She had to go on duty by launch, and so had a uniform issue of oilskin and sou'wester.

She said 'I had of course to collect my uniform when I enrolled, and I shall never forget struggling home from the Barracks with the rough serge coatfrock, very heavy greatcoat, heavy boots and shoes, woollen ribbed stockings and so on.'

Some found themselves doing things they had never done before. Dorothy Gaitskell (now Ashton) was recruited as the Director's orderly at Great Stanhope Street, straight from a sheltered background. One of her duties was to answer the telephone — an instrument she hated — and another to lay fires.

'One day Edith Crowdy, the Deputy Director, saw me and said "Have you ever done this sort of thing before?" I had to confess I hadn't. She set to and showed me how to lay a fire. They were all very kind.'

Laura Newbery bought a single ticket from London to Portsmouth and joined in April 1918. She was prepared to do anything and was taken on as a steward. This was a joke at home as she was reputed to be completely undomesticated and not even able to boil an egg.

Winifred Shawyer (now Drudge) and her sister Eileen who served at the seaplane station at Bembridge, Isle of Wight, helped to make up a WRNS football team. They had a male goal-keeper and male opponents played with their hands tied . . .

Three sisters of whom Victoria Frater was one, joined as immobiles at the Crystal Palace in 1917. She became a despatch rider: 'Our officer, Vera Laughton, picked me with others for Wren advertisement photographs which went all over the world.

'A very large picture of me hung at the National Gallery, London. Many years later, when she was Dame Vera, she introduced me to Prince Philip at a reunion.'

Drivers had a lively time. Margaret Bassett (now Holroyd) at the London garage in Albany Street, was chosen as Admiral of the Fleet Earl Jellicoe's personal driver for three months, while he was at the

Admiralty. 'I used to meet him at Waterloo every morning, then wait on him all day, and return him in the evening. He had so many appointments and meetings, but he was very thoughtful and considerate — truly of a dying breed.'

She noticed that many drivers would only drive what they were used to or had learnt on, so she determined never to refuse a job, and drove anything from a solo motor-cycle to a three-wheeler 'large box arrangement, commandeered from milliners who used them for delivering the large hats', vans, small lorries and every kind of car.

There were hazards: in those days the brakes did not stop the car: 'the back wheels were covered with metal studs which were all very good on a wet road but on wooden paving the wheels just went on.'

Sir Oswyn Murray's cousin, Hilda Buckmaster, reported to Wormwood Scrubs RNAS Depot in January 1918, 'where I was let loose on a Bedford ambulance.' The men did not welcome the WRNS: 'For every job taken over by a Wren meant that a man was released for sea service — and by 1918 few had any stomach for further fighting.

'So we were discouraged: this took such forms as disconnected terminals, air let out of tyres, water in the petrol tanks, and so on.'

Later she went to the Admiralty Garage: 'Mostly I did stand-by railway station duties but sometimes even that had its lighter moments. One day, hurrying along the Euston Road, I did a magnificent skid, turning a full 180 degrees. My Naval officer passenger leaned forward and said, "What a pity there's no music" and "Do you reverse?" '

Loveday Tupper (afterwards Paton, who died recently) was driver to the Senior Naval Officer, Leith Dockyard, and remembered going out in a tug to look at the German Fleet sailing to surrender: 'Our ships looking quite beautiful, spick and span, the Germans filthy, and no one visibly on deck.'

Christine Stewart-Tough remembered the surrender of the German Fleet too. She was on duty at Granton when the signal giving the Fleet's time of arrival, to anchor off May Island, arrived.

'Some days later, after appeals to the Admiral (who had hesitated because of minefields), we were taken out and sailed round the Germans. The sailors looked a trifle astonished. When later they scuttled off Scapa Flow we took it as a personal affront.'

She also visited the German submarine UB11 at Leith, and saw the note in her log book claiming the sinking of HMS HAMPSHIRE with Lord Kitchener on board. [HMS HAMPSHIRE had been thought to have struck a mine.]

Off duty moments provided memories too. May Pitt (now Inggs), a Royal Marine Wren at Eastney, remembers water polo in the RM swimming baths, swimming contests and fortnightly dances.

For G. D. Jackson at Portland memories included a strictly illegal run across the harbour for herself and another officer with coastal motor boat officers 'to show off how well they handled their boat.' But it broke down, they got smothered in black grease, were utterly exhausted, and terrified that they would not get in before the harbour boom was lowered, and would lose their commissions in disgrace.

'We just scraped in but it took us some time to get over the fright.'

She also remembered a party given by the American Fleet to which 500 Wren ratings were bidden. One hundred went from Weymouth, others were brought in from Portsmouth, to drink hot, sweet tea and eat thickly iced cakes, the like of which they had not seen in years.

Queenie Bishop (Lowe) remembered taking part in variety shows, staged by the men, who created 'turns' in which Wrens could take part.

An abiding memory is the hatred some ratings felt for their uniform, finding it unflattering. Some said they resented the officers for being so smart while the ratings were 'such frumps'. Others were proud of it, 'the skirt dashingly short, eight inches off the ground', said Hilda Buckmaster. 'The round pudding basin was copied from the headgear of the Royal Yacht Squadron' she claimed.

Other girls were lining up at sick bay for treatment for rough and inflamed necks where the hard serge had chafed.

Some still remember the attitude of the men amongst whom they worked. As already mentioned, some men resented the Wrens. Jane Rossiter worked with an elderly Chief Writer and two men petty officers: 'In spite of some prejudice against women taking the place of Service men, everyone in that office, and in fact the whole ship's company, was most respectful, kind and helpful.'

Winifred Glew was a tiny supply rating, who came in for a lot of teasing. She will never forget a man driver tipping her one day into a bin of lentils just as the bo'sun's whistle signalled Captain's Rounds.

There was no time to extricate her, the lid had to be firmly shut. Much later she was unceremoniously pulled out, more worried about the possible reactions of her father (a Chief Petty Officer, who luckily never found out) than about smothering by lentils.

Then there was the widely accepted story, probably apocryphal, and repeated in a later war, attributed to a Chief Petty Officer Cook: 'Of all the 'orrible things this 'orrible war 'as done, these 'orrible women are the worst.'

He was very reluctant to part with his Wrens when the time came.

Dame Katharine Furse told the story of the CPO Writer at Weymouth who complained that the women were so slow at picking up ledger work: 'I asked him how long it took a Writer to do so and he replied "Seven years"!'

But perhaps Admiral Sir James Startin was more typical. He commanded at Granton and was horrified when first told that girls were coming to his base. Eventually he accepted the inevitable and decided they must have the most thorough training possible. They took over his Intelligence Office in due course completely.

Granton was the centre for North Sea convoys, and 'Q' ships operated from the harbour.

There was a farewell dinner for the base staff in an Edinburgh hotel in 1919 and at it the Admiral said: 'If I have the honour of ever serving His Majesty again I shall make only one stipulation, which is that I may have Wren Intelligence Officers.'

7

BETWEEN THE WARS: 1919-39

THE REPRESENTATION OF THE PEOPLE ACT was passed in February 1918, giving the vote to all men aged 21 and over, and women aged 30 upwards. This enfranchised eight million new voters of whom six million were women.

There were outraged protests from women in the Services and war work, in their twenties, who felt their part in the war effort entitled them to a vote just as much as a man. Vera Laughton wrote in *Blue Tapestry* many years later: 'I was extremely annoyed to find myself excluded.'

It was not until 1928 that women of 21 and over could vote, although the first woman Member of Parliament (the Viscountess Astor) was elected in 1919.

'A land fit for heroes' was promised by the Prime Minister, Lloyd George. There was no mention of heroines and it proved anyway to be much like any other promise by a politician. For women the post-war world was still prejudiced against them, they met discrimination in employment, further education, and the management of their affairs — they had to have a male guarantor, for example, before they could open a bank account.

The exact total of War casualties may never be known but those killed who came from the British Empire (including Ireland and India) was said to be 1,089,000. It followed that there were many surplus women — widows and spinsters — who had to support themselves (and sometimes their children too), carve out their own life pattern, and provide as best they could for their old age (for this was before the Welfare State as we know it).

Sir Auckland Geddes (now Minister of Reconstruction) set up a women's advisory committee in December 1918 to look at ways of employing ex-Service women. Dame Katharine Furse was on it.

They considered domestic service, an organisation like the men's Corps of Commissionaires, migration — the women to get the same facilities as men for going to the Dominions; but it really was an insoluble problem.

A Society for the Overseas Settlement of British Women was formed, with Isabel Crowdy as its first secretary, and this remained in being for some 40 years.

There was talk of a Women's Reserve. Somehow Winston Churchill was interested in it, and referred to it in the House of Commons. On March 17, 1920, Dame Katharine wrote to him.

'Women are clamouring for this and it seems a great pity not to keep up some organisation in order to be ready in case they are wanted again.'

Nothing came of it nor of Sir Eric Geddes' somewhat strange idea that he could employ ex-WRNS in a body on an English canal system project.

Olga H. Franklin, a cypher officer in charge of ten others in the Commander-in-Chief's office at Devonport, engaged in highly confidential work, began training as a nurse. Later she joined Queen Alexandra's Royal Naval Nursing Service, and from 1947-50 was Matron-in-Chief.

Another ex-Wren, May Farquharson (now Fuchs), a shorthand typist in the ballistics and experimental offices at HMS EXCELLENT, got a job in Cambridge typing a handbook of AA gunnery, compiled by her wartime officers, now back at their respective universities.

Joan Carpenter, who had been a driver at Dover, eventually became secretary of the Service Women's Club in London, while Dorothy Gaitskell (Ashton) went to stay with her mother in the East, and in due course got married.

On January 20, 1920, Dame Katharine Furse called a meeting at her home, 112 Beaufort Street, Chelsea, 'to consider the proposed formation of an ex-Service women's organisation, with either a separate branch of WRNS members or with WRNS joining a central body'. Those present were Dame Katharine, Miss I. Crowdy, Mrs Jarrett, Mrs Day and Miss Royden.

They formed a WRNS-only organisation, the WRNS Friendly Association, appointed a committee (with the ex-Director as chairman) and set a subscription. By March the association was the Society of Wrens, and by the end of the year it had become the Association of Wrens.

It was formed to keep alive the unique spirit of the Service and to maintain friendships; it also represented the interests of all ex-WRNS on various official bodies such as the Service Women's Fund and the United Services Fund.

(The SWF administered profits in NAAFI canteens returned to the women's Services. The USF was for the benefit of ex-Service men and women and was administered by the Soldiers', Sailors' and Airmen's Families Association.)

The first Association of Wrens committee met on December 16, 1920, at Beaufort Street. By now more people had been drawn in — Hilda Buckmaster, Vera Laughton and Winsome Bull (Kemp) among them. They decided to encourage local branches to form in the old Divisions, with another in the Midlands.

They also started a magazine, *The Wren*, which Vera Laughton agreed to edit — a job she held, with only one break, until 1939. It first appeared monthly, later quarterly, and, more recently, three times a year, and went to every AOW member.

The Association was concerned in the formation of the Service Women's Clubs in London and Edinburgh, and a holiday home at St Leonard's, Sussex.

It adopted HMS WREN and presented her with boat badges. It gave itself a badge, approved by the committee in February 1921, and the new London Branch was invited to look at a suggestion from Miss Waldy (late of the London Hostel) for running a sort of employment agency for ex-WRNS.

In the years between the wars there were inter-Service swimming galas, hockey and tennis matches, camps and rambles. Each year a dinner was held after the annual meeting, open also to husbands and guests. Each Branch arranged a programme of social and fund-raising activities.

Ex-WRNS led the early companies of the Sea Guides (later Sea Rangers)—Veronica Erskine, for instance, started the *Golden Hind* unit, while Vera Laughton began the *Wren* unit, and Dame Katharine was appointed head of the movement.

The General Strike of 1926 was accompanied by rumours of a pending Communist coup in Britain. Then came the great stock market crash of 1931, which brought ruin to many and permanently changed the nation's financing pattern.

The dictators came on the scene soon afterwards and from the mid-1930s there was a growing (and well-founded) fear of a war to come.

Various proposals were made to the government for a women's

reserve corps to provide trained personnel. A special sub-committee was set up in October 1935 to consider this.

Each of the Services was asked to forecast its possible womanpower requirements: the Admiralty reported singularly promptly in November 1935 that most of what they would need could be obtained through labour exchanges, and that no training could be given in peace-time.

The sub-committee concluded that no organisation could usefully be started for the Navy before the outbreak of a war.

In April 1937 the report of the inter-Departmental Committee on the Emergency Powers (Defence) Bill included a section on auxiliary services, and stated that the War Office intended to found a women's corps at an early stage, in the event of war. The Committee considered that the Royal Navy and Royal Air Force would also need women's corps.

Yet another committee report in October 1937 stated that it might be desirable from the start of hostilities for women to be enrolled in a uniformed corps, supervised, organised and disciplined under the Admiralty's direction.

On October 13 Dame Katharine told the AOW committee that she had written, as President, to the Admiralty to offer the services of ex-WRNS should the need arise. The Admiralty replied that the use of women in time of emergency was 'receiving careful consideration'.

She suggested the formation of an advisory group or of 'some sort of reserve ready to expand if required'. The Admiralty said 'This suggestion has been considered.'

Throughout the autumn and winter of 1937 and again in the spring of 1938 she renewed her offers of help. Even the Admiralty began to realise that ex-WRNS were getting restive, seeking some form of definite lead or statement.

A couple of ex-officers had written to the AOW asking if the WRNS would start recruiting independently. As it did not exist at that time, it could not. Many ex-WRNS wrote to the Admiralty or to the Prime Minister's office offering their services.

Having been told that an immediate decision was needed on whether the three Services would draw on a single women's uniformed corps, the Second Sea Lord, the Deputy Secretary of the Admiralty, the Director of Personal Services and the Head of Commissions and Warrants met on May 11, 1938. They decided to adhere to the policy hitherto followed.

No steps were considered necessary for recruiting or training women in time of peace. They conceded that it would be desirable to determine requirements in time of war, and to outline the organisation which would then have to be set up.

It was agreed that recruiting in war would be through the Ministry of Labour, and a meeting with their representatives was held on May 16, followed by a submission to the Second Sea Lord and the Secretary of the Admiralty on May 31. A memorandum was submitted to the full Board of Admiralty.

On July 25 the Board agreed on the number of women required. Apart from those to be in Headquarters, the 1935 estimate of about 3,000 stood. They would be mostly clerks, domestics, motor drivers, charwomen, packers and so on. None of these would need training in peace and there was no need to set up a special organisation.

In peace women should be employed as civil servants. The question of uniform would have to be considered only if it was necessary to put all women working in the Admiralty into it in wartime.

A uniformed service was desirable in the ports, but it would be on a civilian basis — the women would live in their own homes. It might be a good thing to prepare a skeleton organisation and find principal officers to take charge when an emergency arose.

They decided to ask Commanders-in-Chief to give specific details of their requirements, and shortly afterwards a retired civil servant, Mr C. M. Bruce, was recalled to work on a scheme.

Practically the first thing he did in September 1938 was to consult Dame Katharine over the selection of 'a suitable woman to organise the Service'. However no actual move was made.

In the light of Munich and its warning signals, a handbook on *National Service* was published for the general public, and in it appeared the first announcement about the new WRNS.

It gave requirements 'in time of war or emergency' as 1,500 women to substitute for Naval and Royal Marine ranks and ratings in (a) secretarial, clerical, accounting, shorthand and typewriting duties, and (b) domestic duties as cooks, stewardesses, waitresses and messengers.

It stated that those interested in receiving details when ready should apply to the Secretary of the Admiralty (Civil Establishment Branch I).

The handbook was out by the end of 1938 and by April 1939 the Admiralty had received some 20,000 applications for further particulars—only most of those who wrote thought they had, in fact, applied to join the WRNS.

It was nobody's job in the Admiralty to answer these letters and indeed some were never acknowledged.

Some irate ex-WRNS who did not get a reply and did not know there was no staff to reply, wrote again, and when they still heard nothing went off in a huff and joined something else—the FANY for instance. Some who thought they had actually enrolled by writing in, and received no orders, were very angry indeed.

The WRNS new style could be said to date from November 22, 1938, for on that date a paper on the formation and organisation of 'a Corps to be known as the Women's Royal Naval Service' was started, as a result of discussions between the Secretary of the Admiralty (Sir Archibald Carter), Deputy Director Personal Services (P) (Captain M. H. A. Kelsey), the Head of C. E. Branch (Mr A. S. Le Maistre) and Mr Bruce.

Dame Katharine was often consulted and her comments were frequently incorporated. She was informally sounded out about becoming Director but felt that a younger woman was needed, although she would do all she could to help. She had kept all her 1917-19 papers, offered these and put her experience gained then at the disposal of the Navy.

She suggested the preliminary organisation might be done by a small advisory committee of ex-WRNS—Mrs Dakyns, Mrs Wallace, Mrs Wyatt, Mrs Laughton Mathews (the former Vera Laughton) and Miss I. Crowdy. When she was going abroad early in 1939 she wrote to the Secretary of the Admiralty saying that they would be available for advice in her absence.

The Secretary replied immediately: in view of the letters arriving by every post an early meeting to discuss a draft scheme was imperative.

On February 22 this was duly convened at the Admiralty and the two women mentioned by Dame Katharine as possible Directors were there—Mrs Wyatt and Mrs Laughton Mathews—with Sir Archibald Carter, Mr Le Maistre and Mr Bruce.

When they had been talking for a little while, a door opened and the Second Sea Lord, Admiral Sir Charles Little, made an impressive entry, to attend as an observer. The two ex-WRNS present, recalling that the Second Sea Lord had been responsible for the WRNS in 1917, assumed Sir Charles was to be their new lord and master.

They had not realised the significance of the involvement of C. E. Branch. The new Service would be regarded as civilian, not as part of the Navy.

On March 29 Mrs Wyatt told the AOW committee that 'Mrs Laughton Mathews had been invited to a conference at the Admiralty to discuss a scheme for the formation of a Women's Royal Naval Service, the proposed Service to consist initially of non-mobile members resident in Portsmouth, Plymouth and Chatham, and serving as clerical workers, cooks and stewards, messengers and orderlies, and possibly motor drivers.'

At about the same time Mrs Laughton Mathews got a phone call summoning her to the Admiralty. As soon as she and Sir Archibald Carter were sitting, he said: 'Well, Mrs Laughton Mathews, I am instructed by the First Lord to offer you the appointment of Director of the WRNS.'

On March 31 he wrote formally:

> 'Your name has been brought before Their Lordships as a person who could fittingly carry out the duties of Director of this Corps, and I am to request that you will inform them whether you would be willing to take on this responsibility. Should you accept this appointment, you will be given, in due course, full details of the responsibilities, duties and emoluments which accompany the post.'

On April 1 she replied:

> 'I beg you to convey to the Lords Commissioners of the Admiralty my deep sense of the honour they do me in offering me the appointment. . .
>
> 'I am willing to undertake this responsibility and will do my utmost to help in building up a Service that will be a worthy auxiliary of the Royal Navy, and that will uphold the good name of the former Women's Royal Naval Service.'

The Admiralty offered her £600 a year for full-time attendance during the organisation of the Service, and told her that her Deputy had already been appointed – Miss E. M. (Angela) Goodenough, Chief Woman Officer at the Admiralty. They met for the first time when the Directorship was verbally offered to Mrs Laughton Mathews.

On April 12, the day of the Press announcement of the Service's establishment, Sir Archibald wrote again:

'I am commanded . . . to inform you that They have been pleased to appoint you . . . with effect from the 11th instant, for a period of three years, after which period the matter will be further considered. . .

'As such you will be responsible to the Board of Admiralty for the recruitment, efficiency, welfare and discipline of the Women's Royal Naval Service, and your duties will include all matters concerning the entry, promotion, accommodation, medical attendance, pay, allowances, travelling expenses, leave of absence, and retirement or discharge of members of the Service.

'On all these subjects you will communicate as necessary with the Secretary of the Admiralty, and take steps to ensure compliance with such regulations and orders as may be issued for your guidance.'

In *Blue Tapestry*, the new Director wrote years later:

'This document remained as my only terms of reference for three-and-a-half years, with the exception that as soon as the Medical Director General opened his mouth early in 1941, I, with much relief, dropped into it the responsibility for WRNS medical matters.'

The 1935 figure of 3,000 women seems to have been forgotten not only in preparing the 1938 handbook but also in the fuller memorandum for publication, approved in April 1939. Both the last two said 1,500 women were to be recruited.

In the latter statement the age limits were given as 18–45 (later changed to 18–50 and later again to 17½ minimum age). Enrolment and registration would start at once for immobile WRNS at the major Naval ports, and Rosyth was added to the earlier list. Applicants must be British subjects, the daughters of British-born parents.

Three skilled and one unskilled branches were specified – Office Duties, Motor Transport, Cooks and General Duties.

The Director and Deputy Director would be at the Admiralty, with Port Superintendents at the ports; officers would be called Chief Officer, First Officer and Second Officer, while ratings would be Chief Wren, Leading Wren and Wren. Third Officer and Petty Officer Wren came later.

They were promised a uniform of 'distinctly Naval type'.

Office Duties women would be enrolled and trained in peace-time, signing on for four years, and bound to attend 24 drills a year, each of two hours' instruction. They were to be taught how a Naval establishment was run, and familiarised with their war duties. No pay would be given, but each woman completing the 24 drills would get 10s to cover any expenses.

Volunteers for the other skilled branches would be registered for quick call-up but not enrolled or trained. General Duties volunteers would not even be registered.

The Director changed this. All accepted volunteers were enrolled and put into training, and those who had taken this before war broke out were promised uniform at once on embodiment.

Women who thought they might be in 'reserved occupations' were at first warned off, but were later advised to apply anyway when their occupations could be checked.

The pay to be offered 'when finally embodied' looks ludicrous to modern eyes, but it was in line with the prevailing rates of pay in the Royal Navy. It was different from many civilian salaries, and some women made substantial financial sacrifices when they did join.

Chief Officers were to get £275 a year, immobile, and £200 with accommodation if mobile. This was the first mention of mobile women — and mobile service was, in fact, approved only three days before war started.

First Officers were to have £240 (immobile) or £165 (mobile); Second Officers £210 (immobile) and £135 (mobile).

The weekly pay for ratings is best understood in chart form: —

	Unskilled		Skilled	
	Immobile	Mobile	Immobile	Mobile
Chief Wren	40s	20s	43s6d	23s6d
Leading Wren	35s	15s	38s6d	18s6d
Wren	30s	10s	33s6d	13s6d

Commanders-in-Chief were asked to provide accommodation for the Superintendents, who would do the actual work of registration and enrolment, and to arrange for the training of Office Duties volunteers.

Shortly afterwards Royal approval was given for the formation of the Service, the Director's letter of appointment was despatched, a notice sent to the Press, and on the same day, April 12, an Admiralty

Office Acquaint stated that the Director was accommodated in the Admiralty and had taken up her duties.

She had been given a very small room, with one alongside for a secretary—there was little or no furniture, no typewriter and no typist.

She was told that her first task was to go with the Deputy Director to Chatham and Portsmouth to see how the WRNS could help the Navy, both in peace and in war (which was now accepted as inevitable).

But there were those huge sacks of unanswered mail and more letters coming in by every post.

Several members of the Association who lived in or near London were practical. They telephoned immediately to ask if there was any way in which they could help. One got the reply: 'Oh yes, please come and help me with all these letters.'

Beatrice Browne put on her hat and coat, caught the next train from Upminster, and set to work. There were others; they were all volunteers, enthusiastic but largely without office experience. But they did a splendid job.

An early recruit was Lady Cholmondeley who was appointed Staff Officer at Headquarters, providing oil for the wheels of administration in her inimitable way and contributing much to the maintenance of high standards.

8

THE WRNS RE-FORMED

APPLICATIONS WERE INVITED for the posts of Port Superintendent from women living in or near the major ports. They had to be aged 35 and upwards, were to be responsible for recruitment, efficiency, discipline and well-being of the women serving in their areas, and therefore to have had some experience of organisation concerning women and girls.

The salary offered was £365 a year, fulltime, with a peacetime retainer of £1 per day of actual attendance. The closing date was April 22.

The selection board comprised the Director and Deputy Director, Miss Myra Curtis (whom Mrs Laughton Mathews found formidable but a tower of strength) and Miss L. F. (Nancy) Nettlefold, a director of Guest, Keen and Nettlefold, who had been at university with the Director. She had been on the Equal Pay Commission (did anyone think this was a phenomenon of the 60s and 70s?).

Out of 700 applications three women were chosen who were to prove in every way worthy officers and leaders of the new Service. Joan Carpenter went to Chatham, Muriel Mackenzie-Grieve to Rosyth, and Mrs E. V. Welby was appointed to Plymouth. It proved difficult to find the right person for Portsmouth but in due course Amy Curtis was appointed.

A Chief Officer was appointed at Portland, and prospective recruiting officers found for Bristol, Cardiff, Dover, Deal and Liverpool. There were plans, but not yet the people, in commercial ports like Hull.

Mrs Laughton Mathews wrote: 'Prior to the outbreak of war I was in fact given no instructions to prepare anything but a Service which would work on voluntary lines in peacetime.'

The office was kept open seven days a week, and she and her Deputy alternated their days off. Clerical help from the Admiralty

typing pool and volunteers proved inadequate and the Director asked
for, and got, her own secretary—Miss N. K. Kellard, who had been a
World War I Wren, and was working in the Admiralty. She retained
her throughout the war.

The Director and her Deputy had Dame Katharine Furse's papers
from the earlier war for guidance, but they had to find out what the
Navy would expect, how this could be met, how women would be
recruited, trained, uniformed, drafted, accommodated, fed and
paid.

They had to work out rules and regulations, consider the possible
welfare needs of large numbers of women from different age groups
and social backgrounds, and provide a foundation on which the
Service could expand when the time came.

They were largely left to get on with it, but as the Director sagely
observed, if they had not been doing what was expected of them,
they would doubtless have been told about it.

She seldom saw the Secretary of the Admiralty, or the Head of
Civil Establishments, and she never recalled meeting the man who
was First Lord when she was appointed, Earl Stanhope.

The call-up of men began in May 1939. From June onwards
preparations were going forward in the ports, recruits drilling in their
street clothes, with WRNS armbands.

A number of WRNS were called up from July onwards. For
example, Mrs Noel Horsey, a 1917-19 Deputy Principal, was
appointed on August 23 to Portsmouth as Chief Officer, and sent to
the R.N. Barracks 'to start the Wrens there'.

Through the summer the international situation worsened. People
cut short their holidays, schoolchildren were evacuated from likely
danger areas, sandbags, air raid shelters, trenches and 'black out'
were in readiness.

The British ultimatum to Germany to cease hostilities had its
answer with Hitler's declaration of war on Poland on September 2.

After a thundery night Sunday September 3 was sunny. The
churches were full, and wireless sets were on in most homes—as the
hours slipped away the British Broadcasting Corporation made
frequent announcements of an important statement coming.

The Director WRNS was on her day off, lying in bed reading the
papers, and thinking about getting up to go to church.

The British Prime Minister (Mr Neville Chamberlain) broadcast at
11 a.m., telling the nation it was at war. The air raid sirens

sounded almost immediately. In a tension so great it was tangible, everyone thought this was the German attack, the *blitzkreig* that European nations had experienced: attack from the air preceding invasion.

Senior Admiralty staff, among them the Deputy Director WRNS, were in the First Lord's office, and a minute after 11 a.m., the Principal Private Secretary, Mr E. A. Seal, bowed and said 'Miss Goodenough, I have the honour to inform you we are at war.'

There was no WRNS Headquarters staff, no trained Unit Officers, but there were about 1,000 immobile Wrens, and immediate cries for Wrens from all over the country, not only from the ports but also from the new bases which started up very quickly.

Mrs Wingate had been serving for three days. She believes she was the first Wren on Whale Island, where she was a cook in the officers' galley, and that Mary Lloyd was the second, joining as a steward. This was the same Mary Lloyd who was to become the first Director who had begun her service as a rating.

Doris Hardy had been attending weekly lectures on Naval discipline and procedure at Portland and reported at once. There was no immediate uniform 'and when we were finally issued with it we were not very enthusiastic. . .'

Mrs Horsey received the first batch of 17 Wrens, writers for the Certificate Office and the Drafting Office, at Portsmouth Barracks.

At first she worked at Coronation House, the WRNS Headquarters for Portsmouth Command 'where all was chaos' but after a few weeks moved into the Barracks, the last establishment in the Command (at that time) to accept WRNS.

Fair chaos reigned at WRNS Headquarters too. The Director, the Deputy, two typists and twelve volunteers had been moved into one large room. A screen divided the two senior officers' desks from the hurly-burly, telephones which rang constantly, applicants being interviewed, and waiting queues of other would-be Wrens.

Within a week of moving into that room they were off again, to Kingsway, which meant a long walk or a bus ride every time they wanted to consult anyone in the Admiralty. They had two small rooms, plus a clerk's room, and a large one where 12 officers and some voluntary workers coped with everything from filing to clothing, interviews to drafting.

Mrs Jane Rossiter and Mrs Beatrice Browne, both early volunteers and ex-Wrens, were enrolled with the official numbers 1 and 2. The former became an officer, the latter a Chief Wren (immobile), the senior rating at Headquarters until she retired in 1947.

A later Headquarters move was to Northumberland Avenue, and finally they went to Queen Anne's Mansions, near St James's Park.

Port Superintendents and Unit Officers in other ports were responsible for recruiting local women on an immobile basis, to meet local requirements. In fact women were applying direct to the ports from all over the country, and were being accepted without reference to London.

The estimated officer requirements in the summer of 1939 for four major ports had totalled 131 but when war was declared there were already 220 officers and ratings actually serving in these four.

In May 1940 Chief Officer Jocelyn Woollcombe was brought to Headquarters from her home town of Plymouth to become Superintendent controlling recruiting and entry, and organising training and drafting.

Her title became Deputy Director (Manning) a little later on, and she succeeded Mrs Laughton Mathews as the first post-war Director.

There was a delay until New Year before uniforms were issued. The first proposed design, based on an outfit worn by a keen Headquarters messenger, of a skirt with jumper top and sailor collar, caused consternation among WRNS when a photograph of it appeared in a national newspaper.

However a navy blue coat and skirt, white shirt with semi-stiff collar and black tie, was adopted. Winston Churchill, then First Lord, called it 'practical and dignified.'

With it went at first a pull-on hat, which was not at all flattering, but was replaced in 1942 with a round sailor hat. The officer's tricorne hat was copied for Chief and Petty Officer Wrens. In certain categories and under certain conditions, berets were worn. Ratings wore an HMS tally band on their hats, and Royal Marine Wrens wore the globe and laurel badge instead.

King George VI visited Portsmouth in December 1939 and expressed surprise at inspecting WRNS who were not yet in uniform. He saw the cooks (mostly sailors' wives or daughters) but thought galley work too rough for women.

It is interesting that the first mobile ratings drafted were four cooks, sent to the RN Auxiliary Hospital, Barrow Gurney. They were closely followed by four telephonists, sent to the Naval Control Service, Southend.

By the early months of 1940 WRNS were serving in places such as Ramsgate, Helensburgh, Lympne, Bristol, Cardiff, Blyth, Dover, Deal, North Shields, Kirkwall, Milford Haven, Swansea, Greenock, Hove, Newhaven, Dartmouth, Belfast, Larne, Yarmouth (Isle of Wight) and Falmouth. There might be as few as six in a unit—but they were immensely proud of 'being in the Navy'.

That, however, was not what the Navy itself thought.

A request from the Director for WRNS to be treated in Naval hospitals brought the ruling that, while slight casualties and cases of sickness, could be treated in Naval sick bays it would be better to use civilian hospitals and doctors. WRNS sick at home should be treated by Admiralty Surgeons and Agents (civilian doctors so appointed).

Naval establishments with a large number of WRNS could have a VAD working to the Medical Officer in the sick bay, and WRNS Hostels (it was some time before officialdom could bring itself to call them Quarters) should have a sick bay, manned with either Naval or civilian personnel.

The Service was not brought under the Naval Discipline Act either, despite the Director's active support of such a move.

WRNS could already be, under their own disciplinary code, discharged, disrated, suspended from duty without pay, have pay deductions for improper absence, be reprimanded, have leave stopped, be given extra work, and have privileges restricted.

The only other punishments under the Act were imprisonment and detention, and these, the Navy said, were 'repugnant'.

The spirit of the Service was considered sufficient to ensure a high standard of behaviour, and as the nature of the contract was civilian it was not considered right that Naval regulations should be imposed.

As the weeks of the 'phoney war' lengthened into months the WRNS intake rose from 200 a month to 800. By the end of 1940 there were 10,000 officers and ratings.

In an Admiralty Fleet Order of October 1939 the first list of categories appeared, under Specialised and General Duties heads. The former included secretary, cypherer, coder, clerk, accountant, typist, shorthand typist, telephone operator, signaller, motor transport driver and cook. The latter covered steward, messenger or orderly, waitress, house maid, kitchen maid and laundry maid. Lines of demarcation were not as clear in the beginning as later. A job had to be done and those on duty did it.

Cooks were to become the third largest category. The first came in already trained but from 1940 they were offered training in a Naval cookery school before starting duty.

The early telephone and teleprinter operators were GPO-trained, but were later trained by the Navy and had their own specialist officers. The first Wren wireless telegraphists went on course in January 1940, emerging that summer as the first Chief Wren special W/T operators, with some of the first on duty at Rosyth.

The first four plotters were employed at Dover in the summer of 1940, with plotter officers around from 1941. There were 234 drivers in late 1940, driving lorries, vans or staff cars; initially nothing over one ton but later vehicles of up to three tons.

Despatch riders were working with Naval riders at the Admiralty in late 1939 but by the following Spring had replaced the men entirely. Later that year there were D/Rs also in Portsmouth and Liverpool.

Parachute packers had their first course at Yeovilton early in 1941, and a year later ratings went on the first officers' course at Eastleigh. The first recorders on the degaussing ranges were at Helensburgh in the Spring of 1940. By the end of the war they had been employed at every range in the country where women were allowed, and had also served overseas.

Writers engaged on pay work were a separate category by mid-1940. Supply ratings went on courses from June 1940 to learn the ways of the Navy in kitting, checking of invoices and accounts, issuing of stores and so on.

From 274 officers in three branches in 1939 to 561 by December 1940 was another indication of how numbers were rising. By the same date WRNS were serving in almost all Naval establishments and bases in England, Scotland, Wales, Northern Ireland and even in the Orkneys.

The first to go there were stewards, writers and messengers in November 1939. The first communications ratings followed in the summer of 1940 when accommodation was ready at Kirkwall, and other Wrens went to Thurso and Hatston.

Belfast formed the first Northern Irish unit in December 1939 with immobile clerical and communications personnel. Larne and Londonderry followed.

The first recorded volunteers for overseas service were members of the accountant and clerical staff at the RN Air Station, Ford, Sussex, who offered to go with the Observers' School to Trinidad in the

autumn of 1940. But then it was decided that locally recruited staff
would be taken on instead in the West Indies.

From early 1941 the Service expanded enormously. Categories were
introduced which were far from being the sort of work generally
associated with women. Radio and air mechanics, maintenance,
torpedo-women and boats' crew, for instance.

From the beginning the Director had held the view that, given
training, women were perfectly capable of undertaking most shore
duties in place of men. Not everyone agreed with her, but the need
for WRNS and yet more WRNS, and the growing amount of work to
be carried out by women, ensured that this training was made
available.

In January 1941 the first overseas draft went to Singapore – 20
Chief Wren special W/T operators and a Second Officer. Soon
afterwards another followed, and during the year drafts went to
Washington and Singapore.

In time Wrens were also to go to South and East Africa, the
Mediterranean and Levant, Australia, India and Ceylon, Hong
Kong, and North West Europe.

The loss of the whole of the first draft en route to Gibraltar when
the troopship, ss AGUILA was torpedoed, was a tremendous shock.
Twelve cypher officers and 10 Chief Wren special operators (and a
Naval nursing sister) were killed instantly. Their slow little ship was
in convoy – the first to be attacked by a U-boat pack.

Miss Goodenough telephoned the Admiralty immediately asking
for news of any survivors. The Director, who had personally
interviewed the draft, and seen them again just before they sailed,
was inspecting units in Plymouth when she was told. Afterwards she
could never think of the loss without also thinking of summer in the
West Country.

There were a few survivors, including the captain (who was
torpedoed again on his way back to England). He visited the Director
on his return.

Future WRNS drafts going overseas were allowed to travel in HM
ships, sometimes taking duty on board during the voyage, or in large
troopships. This did not prevent losses.

The Rev. Charles de Candole was a Naval chaplain. He was with a
draft of 60, including 40 WRNS, embarked in ss ORBETER (an RAF
trooper) which sailed in December 1943 in the first convoy to sail
through the Mediterranean and through the Suez Canal.

In South Africa the Wrens left to join another troopship for Colombo: 'You can imagine our horror when later we heard they had been lost. Only two of the Wrens survived.'

Angela Hadland (now Dawe) was torpedoed in the Mediterranean, and picked up from a lifeboat by a United States destroyer. Mollie Baugh got through safely to India where there was a collection to help a draft, in a following convoy, to replace their belongings — all a total loss.

Moira Grey (now Anderson) remembered a different experience. She was one of 20 officers on board MARNIX VAN DER SILT ALDEGORDE in November 1943, when it was torpedoed and sunk, again in the Mediterranean. They were eventually put ashore in North Africa and a week later were on their way to India, to join Lord Louis Mountbatten's staff.

She said: 'I have never seen or read any reference anywhere to this troopship, maybe because not one of the 1,000 troops in her were lost.'

In June 1942 Third Officer Audrey Coningham's ship was torpedoed. After 15 minutes' swimming in the sea, she saw two seamen clinging together, one in a lifebelt which he was using to support the other. They assured her they were all right, but a little later she saw they were in difficulties and swam over to them.

She took off her own lifebelt, and with the help of a man who was swimming, lifebelt-less, nearby, gave it to the seaman in difficulty. Then she swam to a ship in the vicinity and was picked up. Both seamen were also rescued. For that bravery she was Mentioned in Despatches.

By the end of 1942 there were 211 officers and 741 ratings serving overseas in eleven establishments.

In the British Isles there were 1,775 mobile and 26 immobile officers and 26,616 mobile and 9,938 immobile ratings, serving in seven Commands — Nore, Dover, Plymouth, Portsmouth, Rosyth, Orkneys and Shetlands, and Western Approaches.

9

THE BUILD-UP

THE WRNS WAS SUCCESSFUL, and expanding so rapidly, that there were those in the Royal Navy who considered the time had come to take it over and run it themselves.

The Director was prepared to admit that some instructions could be up-dated, and that in some ways — from a Naval angle — the Service was run in an unorthodox way.

She contended however that the organisation, built up for and with the Service, was better for the women in it than if it had been run on Naval lines or by the men.

A significant decision had been taken in April 1941 when the WRNS ceased to be part of Civil Establishments and became part of Naval Personal Services.

However in mid-1942 the Admiralty set up a committee to consider WRNS administration, with Rear Admiral H. Walker, Director of Personal Services, as chairman.

Mrs Laughton Mathews prepared and presented papers on Administration and Regulations, which the committee amended in some places, but recommended as the official Orders.

In its report it recommended all the points for which she was trying to get approval (and so saved months of negotiation). The most important decision was that the WRNS should be run in every respect at all levels by women.

As the Director WRNS put it, they had been obliged to prove themselves, and largely left to work out their own salvation. Having done so, and with the committee's report behind them, the Admiralty's attitude was 'very generous'.

The scope of work done by Wrens continued to widen. Radar detection finders, cinema operators, gunnery dome operators, recruiters, submarine attack teacher operators, meteorological duties, bomb range markers, vision testers, cine gun assessors, AA target

1 The Director, Dame Katharine Furse, dictates replies to letters in her office at Great
Stanhope Street to her secretary, Miss Butcher.   (*Lent by Lady Ashton*)

1917–19 World War One

2 A happy group outside WRNS Headquarters in Great Stanhope Street, London. The
Chief Section Leader's uniform is very similar to those of later years. The rating on left was
in signals, according to her category badge.   (*Lent by Lady Ashton*)

3 Physical jerks for new entries, World War One style. Scene in a wintry mist which failed to dampen enthusiasm or hide some nifty ankles. (*Lent by AOW*)

4 The Secretaries' room at WRNS Headquarters, Great Stanhope Street, contained furniture and typewriters of a variety which would become familiar also to the World War Two generation. (*Lent by Lady Ashton*)

5 'Did he say turn right?' New Wrens drilling and undecided about which was the right foot and which the left.

(*Lent by Mrs Fuchs*)

6 The Director (fifth from right) and her Headquarters officers. (*Lent by Lady Ashton*)

7 The care and storage of signal flags was a World War One job for Wrens.
(*Imperial War Museum*)

8 WRNS cooks preparing dough and baking loaves of bread in a Naval galley.
(*Imperial War Museum*)

9 Keeping navigation lamps clean and polished ready for use was another job undertaken by Wrens to free men to go to sea.
(HMS Dauntless Collection)

0 Three WRNS drivers (they were Section Leaders) with a light lorry as frequently driven by women.
(HMS Dauntless Collection)

11 Wren ratings who repaired mine nets seen in one of HM Dockyards. Note the tough gloves to protect hands from coarse wire.
(*HMS Dauntless Collection*)

12 Working on mines in one of HM Dockyards these early Wrens had not yet got their uniform.
(*HMS Dauntless Collection*)

13 Wrens cleaning depth charges
    in a typical workshop at
    Lowestoft.
        (*Imperial War Museum*)

14 Wrens with a load of floats
    used with mine nets—the care
    of which was one of their tasks.
        (*Imperial War Museum*)

15 Wrens go off watch at the RN
Barracks, Portsmouth.
(*Lent by Mrs B. Browne*)

16 A day at sea—in brisk weather—for officers and ratings of the WRNS. With s
on the deck of HMS *Orion* was a somewhat queasy-looking member of the shi
(*Lent by*

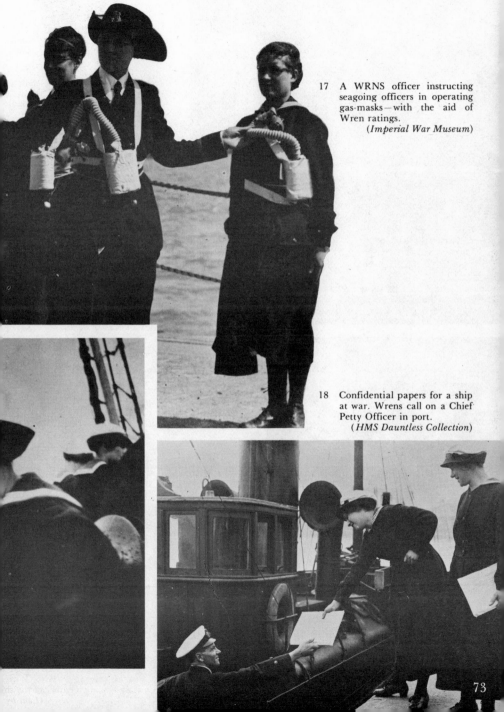

17 A WRNS officer instructing seagoing officers in operating gas-masks—with the aid of Wren ratings.
(*Imperial War Museum*)

18 Confidential papers for a ship at war. Wrens call on a Chief Petty Officer in port.
(*HMS Dauntless Collection*)

19 Like many World War One drivers, it was Mrs White's job in 1918 to take senior officers around ports, to and from ships and railway stations, and to attend important meetings.
(*Lent by Mrs Holroyd*)

20 Store keepers and boat cleaners at a coastal motor boat base in 1918. The head gear protected long hair from becoming entangled or getting covered in grease. Trousers were an innovation too.
(*Lent by Mrs Ball*)

21 Those were the days—Wrens off-duty on Southsea beach posed happily for the camera. This was, for the time, quite a daring 'snap'.
(*Lent by Mrs B. Browne*)

22 'Heave!' A PT instructor encourages a Wren tug-of-war team watched with partisan interest by a Naval audience.
(*Lent by Lady Ashton*)

23 The WRNS marching in the 1919 Peace Parade in Central London, with the Director at their head, her senior officers behind her. A scene that stirs the heart almost 60 years later.
(Lent by Lady Ashton)

24 The Peace Parade saw a big WRNS contingent marching smartly along the decorated route. The Admirals of the Royal Navy who were watching spontaneously applauded as the Wrens went by.
(Lent by Lady Ashton)

25 Miss Vera Laughton was in charge of the WRNS Central Training Depot at Crystal Palace. A journalist, she later edited *The Wren*, and in 1939 became the Director of the re-formed WRNS.
(Lent by Mrs Frater)

26 Peace at last! A Peace Night dance in 1919 where all ranks of the Royal Navy, Royal Marines (Red and Blue) and WRNS (in welcome civilian dress) celebrated.
(Lent by Mrs B. Browne)

27 King George VI inspecting the Wren cooks at Portsmouth in December 1939, escorted by First Officer (later Chief Officer) I. N. Horsey, who served in both wars. The King thought galley work too hard for women, but these, the womenfolk of sailors, were early members of what became the third largest category of Wrens in World War Two.

(Portsmouth & Sunderland Newspapers)

1939-45 World War Two

28 The epoch-making day when uniform was issued. New entries at HMS *Cochrane* receive theirs in early 1940 — some of the first Wrens to be fully equipped. All that remained was to ensure that it all fitted!

(HMS Dauntless Collection)

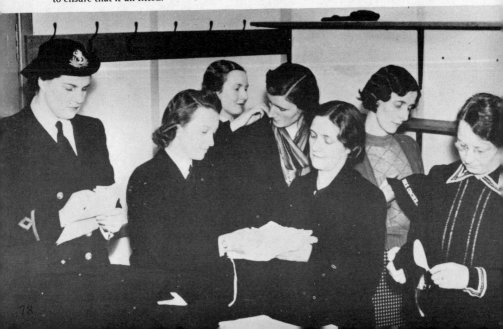

29 The staff of the WRNS Drafting Office in the RN Barracks at Portsmouth in 1940. A number of the women wore berets — and those at the back of the group had not yet even got uniform. Many of these Wrens were immobile, living in their own homes.

(Lent by Mrs Horsey)

30 'Take cover!' Air raid practice at Portsmouth in 1940. This major port was to be badly damaged by bombing, and many members of the WRNS were killed and injured. The smiles of this picture were soon replaced. *(Portsmouth & Sunderland Newspapers)*

31 A little-known job for the
Wrens—coaling ship, working
alongside men, wielding a
shovel with the best of them.
   (*Lent by 1/O P. Williams*)

32 The only Wren blacksmith—
Leading Wren (believe it or
not) Smith.
   (*Lent by Cdr Compton Hall*)

33 A driver at HMS *Drake* carries out running repairs to her lorry. She had to be able to cope with most servicing, except really heavy work. WRNS drivers were vital in the build-up to D-Day.
   (*HMS Dauntless Collection*)

34 A WRNS despatch rider gets mechanical assistance from a Naval rating. Despatch riders such as Pamela McGeorge drove through blitzes to deliver messages: in her case, at Plymouth, she defied bombs to earn the BEM.
   (*HMS Dauntless Collection*)

35 The Wrens at Great Yarmouth
had a successful band — which
the sailors were secretly very
proud of, although they might
have looked (officially) slightly
askance!

(Lent by Mrs Nettleton)

36 The Duchess of Kent inspecting Wrens at St. Budeaux,
Plymouth. In the group behind
her is First Officer M. Drummond, the unit officer, and
later to be Director.

(HMS Dauntless Collection)

37 Sunday April 11, 1943 — the fourth anniversary parade of the re-formed WRNS marches past the Queen on a dais outside Buckingham Palace. With Her Majesty were the Chief Commandant, the Duchess of Kent, Mr A. V. Alexander, First Lord, Admiral Sir Andrew Cunningham, First Sea Lord, and the Director.
   (*HMS Dauntless Collection*)

38 Dame Vera Laughton Mathews greeted by Headquarters staff on returning from her investiture at Buckingham Palace in 1945.
   (*HMS Dauntless Collection*)

39 Boat's crew Wrens handled many kinds of small craft in harbours and coastal waters — and some were even trained as pilots to take ships across the Channel after D-Day (1944).
(*HMS Dauntless Collection*)

40 WRNS signals officers and ratings went to sea regularly aboard the famous liner *Queen Mary*, handling highly confidential messages and similar work. (*HMS Dauntless Collection*)

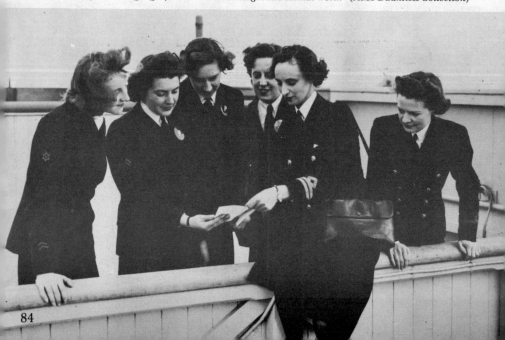

41 The German Navy surrenders—and a Wren boat's crew is on duty as a German E-boat commander leaves HMS *Beehive* at Harwich, after discussing terms, escorted by a British officer. *(HMS Dauntless Collection)*

42 The Peace Parade of 1946—the WRNS contingent marches past Their Majesties The King and Queen, the Princess Elizabeth, and the commanders of the Services. *(HMS Dauntless Collection)*

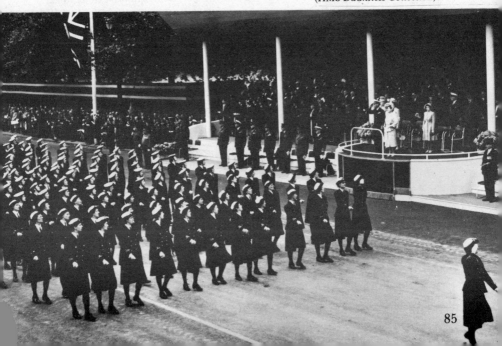

43 HMS *Wren* entering Portsmouth Dockyard on completion of her last commission. Dame
Vera and Chief Officer Broster on the dockside.

(Evening News & Hampshire Telegraph, Portsmouth)

1946–77 Post War

44 'Girls — he's here!' Dame Vera Laughton Mathews thus introduced HRH the Duke of
Edinburgh when he attended the 40th anniversary Wrens' Reunion, minutes after he had
inspected this guard of honour escorted by the Director, Dame Elizabeth Hoyer-Millar.

(Lent by the AOW)

45 Aberystwyth beach on the sunny day in 1952 when a lifeboat given in memory of the WRNS draft, lost on passage to Gibraltar in SS *Aguila* in 1941, was handed over.

(Lent by AOW)

46 Admiral of the Fleet the Earl Mountbatten of Burma, who had many Wrens on his staffs in World War Two, celebrates with members of the WRNR, London Division, after presenting their communications section with the Mountbatten trophy. (*Crown Copyright*)

47 By picket boat to work—a familiar way for many Wrens in war and peace. Wrens of HMS *Drake* go on duty.
(*HMS Dauntless Collection*)

48 Chief Officer McBride (as she then was: today's Director) stirs the pudding—a pre-Christmas tradition maintained still in the Royal Navy.
(*HMS Falcon photographic section*)

9   Practice in marksmanship for a Royal Marine Wren. The Marine Wrens particularly prize wearing the globe and laurel on their caps instead of a normal tally band.

(HMS Excellent photographic unit, Portsmouth)

Off Duty

0   Wrens using RN Sailing Association dinghies at Portsmouth.   *(HMS Dauntless Collection)*

51 Members of the WRNS on active service in Malta on the staff of the Commander-in-Chief. There was a story of a Naval rating who asked a Wren rating with this tally band: 'How did you get promoted so quickly?' (*HMS Dauntless Collection*)

Service Overseas

52 Wrens get everywhere—in this case Hong Kong, where a WRNR unit was in existence for some years, alongside reserves of the other two women's Services. This picture was taken at a farewell gathering before disbandment. (*Lent by Miss Wallace Turner*)

53 Members of the WRNS serve abroad as part of our NATO commitment and this rating is
in Norway, wearing the Norwegian shoulder flash.   (*HMS Dauntless Collection*)

The Service Today

54 A WRNS officer cadet receiving instruction from the commanding officer on the bridge as
part of her training, based at Dartmouth.   (*Crown Copyright*)

55 Wren air mechanic

56 Air engineer mechanic

61 Stores assistant

60 Communications rating

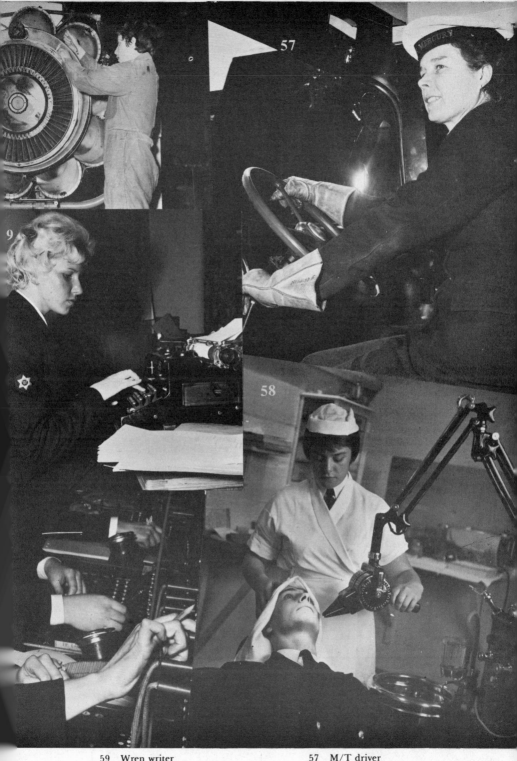

57

58

59   Wren writer

57   M/T driver
58   Dental technician

93

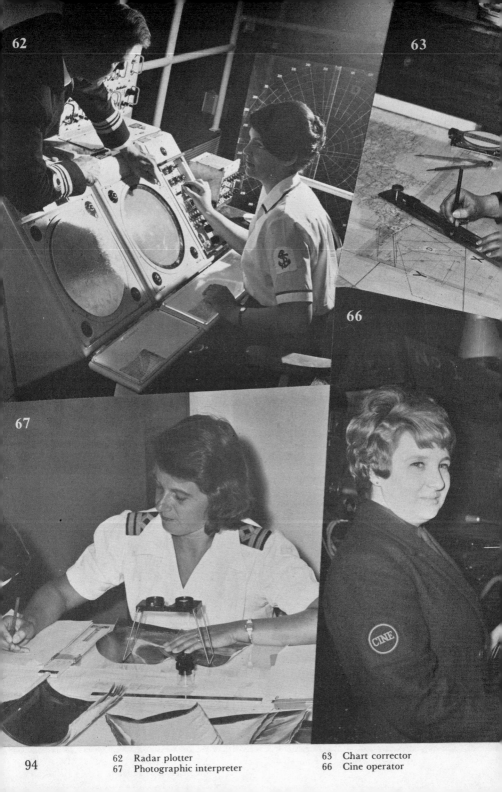

62   Radar plotter
67   Photographic interpreter
63   Chart corrector
66   Cine operator

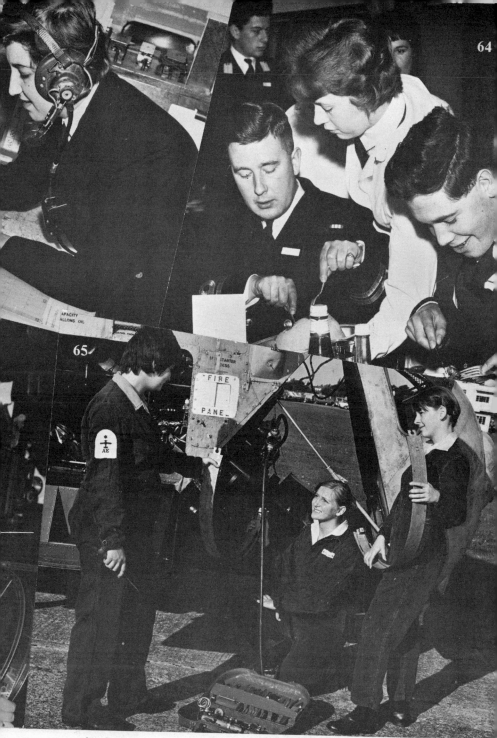

64 Steward
65 Air engineer mechanics

68 The shape of the future? A newly commissioned Third Officer with a Royal Naval Midshipman at Britannia Royal Naval College, Dartmouth, where all officer training for junior staff is now concentrated. (*Charles Risk*)

69 The Chief Commandant, HRH the Princess Anne, Mrs Mark Phillips, speaking with senior ratings in their mess during a visit to HMS *Heron* (Yeovilton). (*Crown Copyright*)

operators, tailoresses, hairdressers, routing officers, orthoptists, and six different categories alone on gunnery sites, and as experimental assistants — all date from about this time.

Officers learning anti-submarine tactics at Western Approaches headquarters in Liverpool were unaware that the 'enemy' against whom they pitted their wits were Wrens in the next room.

Ruth Bryant was an early accountant officer. They replaced men junior accountant officers, appointed for cash duties to shore staffs. She had joined up, aged 35, a chartered secretary who had held a responsible job in civilian life. As a Wren rating she worked on reconstructing the accounts of lost ships. After being commissioned she did similar work at Dartmouth and Bootle, and then went to Australia.

Marjory Plumb's sole desire was to be a radio mechanic (she is now a doctor). The WRNS sent her on a year's course at Battersea Polytechnic, London, and quartered her in the 15th century Crosby Hall, Chelsea. Then she spent six months at HMS ARIEL, Culcheth, Lancashire, became a Leading Wren, was drafted to a Fleet Air Arm station, and issued with a tool kit.

Some Wren mechanics were attached to squadrons, others to the base workshop. They would return to ARIEL for on-training before becoming Petty Officers.

Then there were some Wrens who were in the category of Special Duties (Linguist). These worked on a chain of listening stations, picking up Germans speaking on voice radio, and forewarning convoys and coastal forces of enemy vessels.

Captain Peter Dickens, RN, a coastal forces officer, found their efficiency remarkable. They were very bright girls and excellent linguists, he found.

One of them Pam McKan (now Harding) said: 'We were from varied backgrounds, our common ground being our knowledge of German.'

Familiarity with German handwriting led some of them to work in France and Germany quite early in the Allied Occupation. After hostilities ended Pam McKan worked on the translation of captured enemy documents, and later as an interpreter.

M. A. Rose (now Bleach) had a very unusual WRNS job. In 1940 she was a 20-year-old, working in Foreign Office Intelligence, when a British agent on a special assignment in Gibraltar requested her by name as secretarial assistant. It was just three weeks before a Catalina flying boat landed her in her official unofficial job, by which time she had been turned into a WRNS officer.

After a few months she was moved to Algiers where (against all regulations) her office was on board ship. On one occasion the sea around the vessel burst into flames and she had to leap overboard on to a raft full of chattering Arabs.

She paraded when King George VI inspected the WRNS — with others of HM Forces — on the quayside in the blazing sun. 'How do you keep your uniform so white?' he asked her. In an age of dhobeying not detergents, she replied 'Sunlight soap and blanco, Sire'.

Barbara Treacher (now Greenhalgh) was called a Boom Defence Wren, but was in fact despatching incendiary devices across the Channel from the East Anglian coast. She said: 'Quite a few of us got burnt when the balloons carrying these things caught fire before leaving the ground. I got badly singed on the face and head'.

Violet Tye (now Mills) was called up early in 1944, having hitherto been in a reserved occupation, and hoped to go somewhere full of sailors and the Navy. She became a maintenance Wren, working on landing craft spare parts — at Staines, Middlesex. Later she was at Horsham, but still far from the Navy as such, though there were sailors in the garage which had been taken over as a workshop.

At HMS VULTURE in Cornwall, the WRNS were told they must learn to help defend it in case of invasion. They were issued with World War I rifles and attended compulsory range practice every day.

Joan Williamson (now Baker) found it difficult to cope with the considerable weight of the rifle, tin hat and service gas-mask walking from Quarters to the main block, 'especially when having to salute an officer'.

They took part in an armed night exercise, manning pill-box defences, firing blanks at the Duke of Cornwall's Light Infantry. Not unexpectedly a question was asked about this in Parliament, and the rifles disappeared as suddenly as they had come.

Invasion would have seemed much more likely at Dover, but here in a lull in the shelling and bombing in September 1942, the Wrens held a garden party in the grounds of Dover College. They had all the usual attractions, even a display of vaulting and acrobatics by a local Royal Artillery unit. Later came a dance with cabaret. It was almost a 24-hour long event. Vera Boyce (now Selwood) was, as a

Wren, the principal organiser, and a small profit was given to Service charities.

In November 1942 the Naval Control Service was replacing all RNR officers, in any way suitable for sea service, with WRNS and RNVR officers. Accountant officers were replaced by WRNS counterparts, the confidential book officers had to be women, and the secretary at each unit was, wherever possible, to be a member of the WRNS.

Cypher officers were in particular demand, so much so that there was a chronic shortage, with 'indents' from overseas, and insufficient candidates to meet requirements at home.

Eventually the age limit for cypher officers was reduced to 20 years, provided they had already served for one year, and the qualifying typing speed was reduced from 30 to 20 words a minute. Every possible suitable rating was considered for promotion.

From early 1943 the build-up of forces towards D-Day, the invasion of Europe, dictated where Wrens were to serve. It was the beginning of a massive operation. In the British Isles the greatest demand was from Combined Operations bases and establishments. As the build-up concentrated in the Portsmouth Command so official approval was given for priority drafting for that area, both for new entries, and for those drafted in from other Commands.

Overseas, as the Allies advanced, further WRNS units were set up in North Africa, and existing units enlarged. Others were established in the Persian Gulf, Palestine, Malta, Naples, East Africa, Aden, Ceylon, and India.

There were eight units in the United States where 70 to 75 per cent of the WRNS were locally recruited. 'Local' was interpreted widely: Bermuda, Jamaica, Canada, Newfoundland and Nova Scotia were combed for likely recruits. In the end many came from the British community in the Argentine.

Pat Tiddy was in the second draft which went from the United Kingdom in 1941 to Washington via Canada, in plain clothes. Immediately after Pearl Harbour they emerged in uniform.

They were writers and signals staff, forming the largest group in a joint Services cypher office, dealing with communications relating to ship movements, repairs, stores, and the Joint Staff Missions' planning for future developments in the war.

They were joined in 1942 by British girls from the West Indies and South America, and as more officers were needed, three were

appointed—including Pat Tiddy—from the original drafts. There
was no officers' training, but later probationary Third Officers were
sent to the Women's Royal Canadian Naval Service officers' training
unit.

When Winston Churchill, now Prime Minister, visited the USA
and Canada his cypher staff was augmented by WRNS officers,
drawn from the USA units.

'There were eventually about 50 Wrens on the cypher staff in
Washington, and girls from the Canadian civil service were our
teleprinter operators. We had direct links with the Admiralty and
with the US Navy Department. Our building was the headquarters of
the British Joint Staff Mission and several other British Service
groups: we had a ship's name — HMS SAKER.'

One of the new Commands, brought into being by the war, in
Britain, was Western Approaches, which had a large WRNS staff. It
was 'born' at Plymouth but was based at Liverpool. In January 1941
it had a total of 2,648 WRNS officers and ratings; in January 1943
the number had risen to 10,284. By June 1944 it was at its high peak
of 15,583.

Jocelyn Weeks (now Wheale) went from Plymouth with the first
Western Approaches Wrens. Her job was on the personal staff of the
Chief of Staff. Admiral Sir Percy Noble was the first Commander-in-
Chief, laying foundations for the expansion of the Command, and
the wartime convoy system.

His successor was Admiral Sir Max Horton, a submariner, sent to
pit his wits against U-boat commanders who were being far too
successful.

There was another 'character' at Liverpool, described by Olive
Nicholson (now Wrathall) as 'the famous and never to be forgotten
Captain "Johnny" Walker RN' whose daughter, Gillian, was a Wren.

His ships, among them HMS STARLING and HMS WILD GOOSE, were
invariably given a warm welcome back to Liverpool after their
convoy and anti-submarine achievements.

After just such a return Captain Walker became ill, and died,
worn out by the pressures and stresses of the never-ending watch. He
was given a Naval funeral, the like of which had not been seen in
Liverpool, and would be matched only by the service for Admiral
Horton a few years later.

The signals office was in cellars near the docks, with the
teleprinters, coders, cypher staff, and switchboard. Liverpool was a

prime target for air raids (as were all the big ports). Later there was a signal tower facing the Mersey.

The need for security-mindedness was instilled in every Wren from the earliest probationary training days, reiterated often, and repeated on moving from one job to another. Members of the WRNS were frequently in possession of top secret information, and of otherwise classified material.

As the Service grew larger and the war effort in Britain was being brought to its climax, the chances of passing on highly relevant information were greatly increased.

Most of those girls serving in 1943-44 were young, very few of any age group had experienced anything quite like their service before. They could so easily have succumbed to pressure or subtle enquiry.

It is to their credit that no leaks of information, however inadvertent, throughout the war, could ever be attributed to WRNS personnel.

At Combined Operations Headquarters in London there were officers and ratings with detailed knowledge of raids on Europe prior to the invasion. There were those who took part in the briefings of raid commanders, who knew about secret equipment developed for different purposes. There were those who sent and received signals about secret operations of various types, and those who knew of the failure or success of operations.

Under Vice Admiral Lord Louis Mountbatten (now Admiral of the Fleet the Earl Mountbatten of Burma) as Chief of Combined Operations, all were able to see how their particular work slotted into the whole, for he held regular meetings for his staff of all ranks, ratings and grades.

Joan Joly, however, remembers him for something quite different from secret operations and 'state of war' briefings. She was one of the first four teleprinter operators at COHQ, and on night duty she and another girl were arranging incoming signals in piles, ready for distribution to their various recipients — 'the room looked like a huge card game' — when a young Sub-Lieutenant called in and they all paused for a hot drink.

Suddenly the door opened and CCO himself appeared. The Wrens expected a severe reprimand. They got instead 'a kindly smile and the enquiry "Busy?" '

One of the war's best-kept secrets was a country-based unit, far from ships and water. This was HMS PEMBROKE V or Station X. When they first went there the Wrens were directly under WRNS Headquarters, but local administration was done by the WAAF. The majority of Wrens did not have uniform and were writers.

The first 12 there gradually assumed more responsibility, replacing men, and proving that they could do a job thought to be 'too difficult' for women. By February 1942 they had proved their capabilities, their numbers were increasing, they were replacing men more and more, and they got their own category—SD(X)—but not a badge. What they did proved too difficult to convey symbolically.

During the year the Director WRNS and Superintendent Nore were allowed to visit, and in December the unit was taken over by Nore Command—which was when it was re-named PEM-BROKE V.

Once accepted for SD(X) Wrens were not permitted to transfer to another category except for medical reasons, unsuitability, or on very strong compassionate grounds.

They formed the largest single group working on breaking enemy codes, work which has been described in books about World War II, but without mentioning the WRNS part in it, and on television as recently as early 1977, when a former Wren, Helen Rance, described what her work had been. Much of it is still secret.

M. P. Rowell (now Lewis) said, 'After all these years I find it difficult to believe that we once did this work. The WRNS were the only people actually in charge of the machines and responsible for their efficiency.

'There were always RAF electrical mechanics on duty with us, to maintain efficiency of the machines. However the Wren Petty Officer in charge of each watch was responsible for the information we produced to be sent on to the next relative department in the big chain that made it possible for messages to be de-coded.

'We dealt with all Service information, Army, Air Force as well as Navy and U-boat messages. We were sometimes congratulated and thanked, although at the time we did not, of course, know how we had helped.'

Lady Brind was, as Chief Officer (later Superintendent) Blagrove, in charge of 'P Five'. Her predecessors had been Chief Officer Mackenzie and First Officer Canale—and these gradations of rank were a clue to the increasing importance of the unit.

'The nature of the work of certain sections made this a difficult unit to administer,' she recalled. 'The officers took a great personal interest in the welfare of the ratings in their watches, organised off-duty activities, and kept alive the keenness and enthusiasm in a job which tended to become dull and monotonous . . .'

She commented that a 'great deal of the work undertaken was very highly secret and confidential.' The Wrens who did it were, she considered, not given the rating commensurate with the responsibility they carried, or equivalent to those of the other Services with whom they worked.

But one of the biggest and most difficult secrets any of the Wrens had to keep was that of D-Day.

10

OPERATION OVERLORD

OPERATION OVERLORD involved vast numbers of ships and landing craft, aircraft and men, vast quantities of military equipment, vast planning, a vast back-up organisation, many preliminary reconnaissance raids, and employed the greatest number of Wrens to be concentrated on one project in World War II.

The coastal areas of southern Britain were closed some time in advance of the main operation for security reasons. Wrens could not go home for any reason if this meant leaving the closed area. Mail did not carry their addresses. Special identity cards were issued for use in closed areas.

During the spring of 1944 there was mounting activity. M. E. Barralet was a National Service Wren radio mechanic at Ventnor, Isle of Wight, originally one of a staff of three. As spring advanced a French matelot radio operator joined them, then an ATS sergeant, a team of civil service engineers, and some Marconi experts.

Three huts containing watch rooms went up in the garden of 'The Heights', so did large aerial masts (Miss Barralet had to climb onto the roof to dismantle the old ones) and a direction-finding tower, and then an RAF D/F trailer came.

Everyone worked long hours, and the Island was full of troops, and rumours of Germans invading. In June the troops were suddenly not there any more. A day or two later the Wrens saw the invasion fleet setting out.

Margaret Leach (now Friendship), Petty Office Coxswain in charge of boats' crew Wrens at HMS FOLIOT (a landing craft base near Plymouth) and one of her crew accidentally learnt the date of D-Day some time beforehand. They took security so seriously they did not even report it to their superiors.

A 19-year-old Wren at Newhaven, Nancy Thompson, was one of a large signals staff dealing with a heavy work-load. On the evening of June 5 her watch was taken along the sea-front in a bus, going on duty. There were ships and landing craft on the water, as there had been many times before. But this time there were far more than usual.

She said: 'The watch we relieved were subdued, not as cheerful as usual, and as soon as we saw the signal log, we knew why.

'This was "the longest night", all of us wondering what the next hours would bring to the people across the Channel. Some of the girls were in tears as they had brothers and boy-friends in the invasion forces.

'Before we went off watch the Commander spoke to us all and warned us not to discuss anything that we had seen or heard during the night, under threat of a severe penalty, as thousands of lives were at stake.'

Jean Marston, a driver at Plymouth, was detailed to meet some important officers off a train at Taunton. She found the road blocked by US Marines moving ammunition in convoy. An American military policeman — who had started by being a little fresh — rescued her, and siren wailing, led her to no less than General Sir Bernard Montgomery (later to be Field Marshal the Viscount Montgomery of Alamein) — her 'pick up'.

On a later occasion she took two senior officers to Normandy (a WRNS officer warned her not to go out without a chaperone while in France): 'I had to come back to Plymouth without them as they got killed.'

Moira Shepherd was at HMS HAIG, a Combined Operations base at Rye, Sussex: 'I vividly remember seeing the attacking planes overhead, and the Fleet sailing down the Channel. I even have the six-line letter written to me by my husband on the Normandy beaches on D-Day.'

K. E. Roberts (now Reaney) was on the staff of the Naval Officer-in-Charge, Dartmouth:

'We helped the Americans to set up their teleprinter station and switchboard at the Royal Naval College in preparation for D-Day. Dartmouth Harbour filled rapidly at the beginning of 1944 with American and British landing craft.

'The movement of WRNS personnel through the town was

restricted from the end of May. I wrote on May 31 "Last morning of freedom — 12 noon today is zero hour". From then on the pace hotted up and we were frantically busy.

'In the early hours of Tuesday June 6 there was an uncanny stillness. Then guns rattled the windows. Radio announcements were made all morning. Eisenhower (General in the US Army, commanding the Allied invasion forces, and later President of the USA) and King Haakon (of Norway) both spoke.'

Joanna Finlayson (now Laughton) woke at 4 a.m. on June 6:

'woken by the continual noise of aircraft taking off 100 yards from my window. One by one the engines warmed up, roared across the runways and swept overhead.

'I counted 120 planes in an hour.

'Listening carefully I could hear another noise — the same sound I heard before the raid on Dieppe — the steady burr of ships' engines moving out to sea. D-Day had arrived!

'At breakfast rumour spread — at the office the wireless was on and we heard the first communique from the Supreme Allied Expeditionary Force headquarters: "The AEF has made landings in Northern France."

'The aerodrome was a scene of incredible movement with a tense operational hum about it. Everywhere there were lorries, vans and crash tenders speeding back and forth. Mechanics and fitters crawled around and over the planes, pilots climbed in and out of cockpits, Mustangs were taking off two at a time. They swept along the runways, up and over our heads, while two more swung into position and followed in their wake. The whole flight was up and away in 10 minutes.'

Some of the Lee-on-Solent pilots returned in the evening with time for a quick drink with the Wrens. Many did not.

Olive Newman (now Bird) was at Tower House, Portsmouth:

'Imperceptibly at first but then gaining momentum as the months went by, we realised that a build-up of troops, Commandos, sailors, ships and so on was taking place.

'Inside HMS VERNON itself it was beginning to get chock-a-block with sailors of all nations, landing and mine-laying craft, minesweepers and vessels of all shapes and sizes. Every square inch was taken up with something or somebody, and how they were all housed and fed I shall never know.

'By early June the armada was beginning to assemble in earnest at Spithead . . . I have never seen so many ships together in one small stretch of water and I suppose it never will be seen again.

'For some weeks the harbour area had been completely sealed off and we had to have special identity cards to get into and out of Quarters.

'The weather changed and a southerly gale sprang up which delayed our usual last-thing-at-night look at the ships. When we got up next morning they had all gone. It was almost uncanny.

'From then on for several weeks it was all feverish activity, the huge landing ships coming in empty and going out again laden with tanks, lorries, guns and troops.

'Hundreds of soldiers cheered and waved to the Wrens, probably the last females they saw for some time.'

Enid Best (now Nelson-Ward) recalled 'Absolute silence on the air on the night of June 5/6 until ships were obliged to break W/T silence. Then it was all hell let loose. Coded messages followed one after another. We were so busy I don't remember sleeping at all.'

(She, by the way, later married a descendant of Nelson.)

The Director wrote: 'Someone present described to me the Signal Distribution Office of the Commander-in-Chief, Portsmouth, where some of the Wrens, immobiles of uncertain age, had tears of fatigue running down their faces, yet somehow were carrying on and not making mistakes.'

WRNS and WAAF worked together on the D-Day Plot in Portsmouth Combined Headquarters, into which came top secret information direct from both sides of the Channel and from all ships. The King saw the Plot for himself very shortly afterwards.

First Officer Margaret Drummond (later to be a Director WRNS) was head of section in the office of the Commander-in-Chief, Plymouth, dealing with paper-work for the invasion. Two months before D-Day she received 20 copies of the Naval plan, and almost slept with them.

She and her WRNS staff were responsible for issuing charts, typing and issuing sailing orders, and the allocation of berths to ships. They knew all that was going on.

It was not only these who went to make up the pattern. It was also the drivers, stewards, despatch riders, cooks, confidential book and chart correctors, mail office and censor staffs, supply ratings, boats' crews and many others.

Between May 25 and June 5 WRNS officers acting as censors in the ports dealt with some 400,000 letters. When total censorship was imposed their load was too great, and letters were also sent up to London for censoring.

Between April and June 1944 WRNS supply assistants in one establishment alone—HMS VECTIS, Seaview, Isle of Wight—issuing clothing, food and Naval stores, together with the associated paper-work, dealt with over a hundred ships a day.

Admiral Sir Bertram Ramsay, the Commander-in-Chief, Portsmouth, included them all in his message of congratulation to his Command.

After D-Day, when the climax had perhaps come and gone, the pressures did not let up.

Wren ship mechanics in the South Coast ports, working alongside Naval ship mechanics, were on watch night and day, repairing damaged craft as they returned from the Normandy beaches.

Some boats' crew coxswains were trained as pilots and took smaller ships across the Channel. Two ratings working on chart correcting, kept the charts up-to-date with swept channels and mined areas, for vessels going across to France. (One girl, who put the invasion routes on charts, was actually 'sealed' in the ship where she was working, for ten days.)

At Portsmouth Combined Headquarters there were three wardroom messes (one underground) each serving 800 meals in every 24 hours. The great influx of officers, many staying only briefly, meant that beds had to be made up in caravans and tents, as well as in buildings, and it was Wrens who did this.

It was Wrens, too, who coped with laundering vast quantities of bed linen, and who seemed to be constantly stripping down and making up beds.

In the WRNS mess about 1,200 meals a day were prepared and served, and there was a mid-morning canteen. A two-course supper was provided below ground in five shifts from 2030 to 2300.

It all seemed a far cry from drill practice and lectures on Naval procedure and discipline, from rank and badge recognition, learning to salute, floor polishing and bath scrubbing, and the rest of the probationary Wren's training. It seemed far away from the occasional VIP occasion or parade (such as the WRNS fourth anniversary parade before the Queen at Buckingham Palace).

But it was, after all, what everyone had joined up for — to help win the war.

And the WRNS at home no longer envied the WRNS who had gone overseas.

11

THE WRNS OVERSEAS

FROM FEBRUARY 1943 there had been a Superintendent on the staff
of the Commander-in-Chief Levant (Superintendent J. Frith) with
responsibility for units in North Africa and the Persian Gulf. Then
Superintendent D. Isherwood went to the Mediterranean in June
1944 (and Levant became an Area under a Chief Officer) moving
from Algiers to Caserta to Malta. She was also responsible for WRNS
in Gibraltar.

Superintendent Goodenough left the post of Deputy Director
(Welfare) very reluctantly, to become senior officer in the East
Indies. She died in Colombo of poliomyelitis. She had succeeded
Superintendent A. J. Currie, who had got to Bombay but was then
seriously ill and invalided home.

Miss Goodenough's successor at Headquarters was Superintendent
J. Carpenter.

There were plans for Superintendent J. Woollcombe, Deputy
Director (Manning) to go to the British Pacific Fleet in Australia, but
the war ended first. Thus Chief Officer E. Samuel was in charge of
the WRNS there.

One of the events most often recalled of Middle East service was
the evacuation of Alexandria in 1942, when the German advance
threatened Egypt. The late Superintendent Beryl Lacey (as she later
became) was a Third Officer Quarters Assistant, and wrote home a
very full account of a hectic few days in late June and early July. Only
a fraction of it can be quoted here:

'The atmosphere became pretty tense on Sunday. The telephone
buzzed a good deal but there was no real question of leaving.
The First Officer said would I get in some emergency food in

110

case we had to make a quick flit. I planned what I would buy on
Monday . . .

'Then in the afternoon it was decided that two officers would
go early on Monday as their office was being moved . . . That
really began it as far as we were concerned.

'From early on June 29 it became obvious that offices were
moving—it began slowly and then became more and more
rapid. Sudden demands for laundry, sandwiches, etc. etc.'

The next morning she woke early and packed, hoping she'd forgotten nothing, for she never went back to her room. As soon as she
went on duty she realised it could not be long before they went: 'I was
told that we knew nothing but that when instructions came we would
probably move within the hour.'

Around 1200 orders came. The officers made sandwiches, got a
big tin of biscuits, butter and all the food in the house:

'I was busy shutting things up and tidying up as best I could. I
paid the servants, all the luggage was brought down and taxis
ordered. All piled in and half the luggage was put on an Air
Force truck and went off.

'We arrived in the docks and found everyone boarding an
enormous long train of iron cattle trucks; a few officers in each,
and ratings, with mounds of luggage. There were a lot of
civilians.

'We finally left at 5.25 pm. The heat was frightful . . .'

They were soon hungry but ate sandwiches, and when the light
faded, tried to lie down. The floor space having gone, Mrs Lacey
climbed up onto some luggage:

'The jolting was simply indescribable and from time to time
there were crashes which almost shook one off one's already
precarious and horribly uncomfortable perch.

'Even so we dozed and at 5 a.m. the train stopped. A welcome voice said "All Wrens get out here—this is Ismailia. Go
out of the station—lorries are waiting for you." '

Food, a wash and some sleep were to be had at the YWCA and
after lunch they were loaded into buses and taken to the shore. Two
lighters took them out to the PRINCESS KATHLEEN, once a Canadian
lake steamer.

After a night on board they sailed to Suez, reaching it at 11 am. They stayed on board while rumours flew and everyone got depressed. There were too many civilians and children, who panicked every time an Alert sounded.

After a while Mrs Lacey was sent ashore and instructed to open temporary Quarters. She obtained beds and bedding (but no sheets or towels), a table, two forms and the barest necessities of china. There were no chairs, mirrors or any other furniture.

The bedding proved to be full of bugs. Eventually new camp beds were obtained, which eased the problem. There was running water and electricity but no other amenities.

Margaret Peck (now Heigham) was a Third Officer on board the same ship: 'We had a Chinese crew who went on strike. We had to scrub the decks while they watched. My job was the floor of the bar and I hate the smell of beer . . .'

On her way to Alexandria via the Cape (two months at sea in a troopship) she was one of the first Wrens to go ashore in Cape Town, and still remembers getting her whites ready and putting on white stockings 'that creaked as you walked.' Later, in the Middle East, these were abandoned in favour of bare legs.

Joan Lilley was in the first draft to Malta, G.C. in January, 1944—40 ratings and an officer, few of whom had been outside Britain before.

They were quartered at the Imperial Hotel, Sliema, which also housed civilian families. When the Wrens arrived: 'The entire staff lined up in the hall to welcome us. It was as though we had stepped back into the Victorian era.'

Whenever they left the hotel they were greeted by everyone they met—Service men of all ranks wanting news of home, Maltese shaking them by the hand and welcoming them as deliverers.

'Some of us worked at St Angelo. Our first morning on duty was bright and cold, with a bitter wind, but there were queues of sailors standing outside the clothing store as word had got round that we had brought fresh supplies.

'Many of these men had no shoes or underclothes, just a boiler suit with a blanket round their shoulders. They were survivors . . . We were able to let them have only the essentials.

'I shall always remember that line of sailors, standing there in the bitter cold.'

Priscilla Fuller (now Inverarity) spent some time in Basra, where the heat was intense. There was no air conditioning there in 1943 'and attempts were made to cool the office by "shutters" made of dried leaves, which were splashed by buckets of water by a boy. It didn't have much effect . . .'

She served in the Persian Gulf, Middle East and Ceylon, there becoming an officer. But life was still dominated by coping with life in a tropical climate.

There were the practical details of keeping uniform smart and replacing worn out items, letters to and from home, getting hair done, going to the dentist, or replacing spectacles. The social life relieved what became, once the women were used to living abroad, the dullness of much of the work.

Petty Officer June Foster (now Fisher) went out to India as a member of the Force W staff: 'I joined the Wrens entirely on the strength of reading Katharine Furse's book. There was no kind of influence or pressure from home. But I never regretted it, I loved being in the East, and involved in that war.'

As an Acting Third Officer she was the only member of the WRNS to gain the Indian Independence Medal, having been with Lord Louis Mountbatten when the Supreme Commander became the last Viceroy. She also got the BEM and later the MBE.

The first Wrens to serve in India were at Delhi and Bombay. Later there were others at Coimbatore, Tambaram, Karachi, Calcutta, Madras, Cochin and Vizagapatam.

Mollie Baugh and Audrey Oliver (now Fletcher) recall a Christmas in Kandy when Lord Louis was invited to the WRNS officers' party — and arrived, resplendent, on an elephant.

WRNS went to Sydney, New South Wales, in October 1944, when it was expected that large numbers would be drafted there. By August there were units also at Melbourne, Brisbane and Herne Bay. In addition to clerical and communications categories, there were drivers, cooks and stewards.

In July 1945 a small party was appointed to the staff of the Flag Officer Malaya at Kurunegala — one of them typed the terms of the Japanese surrender — but their work came to an abrupt end when Japan collapsed.

As British and Allied troops moved into Europe the WRNS followed. Enid Best (Nelson-Ward) said: 'We heard we were going to France with ANCXF (Allied Naval Commander-in-Chief Naval

Expeditionary Force). We sailed from Portsmouth to Arromanches, then travelled for miles along dusty roads, past bombed and devastated buildings and empty farms. We sat on the floors of large trucks. We wore navy blue bell bottoms and white tops, with blue braid around the neck and sleeves.'

In St Germain they lived in *apartements* damaged by bombing, and food was scarce. 'From there we moved to La Celle St Cloud, not far from Paris, living and working in the Chateau, a fairy-tale place previously occupied by the Germans. We were some of the first Wrens to go over.'

The first Wrens had arrived on August 15, 1944, to work at Courselles, where the unit eventually numbered 14 officers and 84 ratings.

Then came the party to join the Naval Officer-in-Charge, Arromanches, and at the end of August 45 officers and 146 ratings who had been at Portsmouth arrived at Granville.

The Courselles unit went to Rouen in September, and the Arromanches girls moved to Calais.

Claire Jones (now Jarrett) was Quarters Petty Officer in Calais from December 1944 to July 1945; she was half-French and spoke the language fluently. 'We were mostly supplied with Naval rations but I bought marvellous fresh fruit and vegetables from a little shop nearby. We had a mixture of French and English cooking. We slept on camp beds and because we had no comfortable furniture got 6d a day hard-lying money.'

She added: 'Calais was devastated and our little Wrennery, a small block of flats, was one of the few buildings intact. It was called *Les Roitelets*—the latter being the French word for wren.'

One day the Mayor and his wife were entertained—she was thought to be General de Gaulle's sister—and Petty Officer Jones made croutons to go with the drinks, decorating them with stripes of beetroot—some with the 'V' sign and others with the Cross of Lorraine, the symbol of Free France. This gesture was greatly appreciated by the guests.

In September the ANCXF unit had gone to St Germain-en-Laye, and in January 1945 units were set up in Brussels and Ostend.

On May 2, 1945, the Flag Officer Schleswig-Holstein (Vice Admiral H. T. Baillie-Grohman, serving as a Rear Admiral) and some staff officers, the vanguard of Naval Party 1734 (later to be HMS ROYAL ALFRED) arrived in Germany, but had to wait for the Army to capture Kiel. The Port parties for Kiel, Flensburg, Lubeck and Eckernforde had to make their way by road and arrived after the German capitulation on May 7.

After chaotic weeks in Kiel—badly bombed, full of refugees, lacking any centralised German control for some time and consequently virtually at a standstill—the Admiral's headquarters ship (the Hamburg Amerika's MILWAUKEE) was required as transport and he had to find another 'home'.

This was the German Naval establishment at Plon, to which they moved (as HMS ROYAL HAROLD) and the point at which four WRNS officers joined, on July 29, followed by a further ten.

Rear Admiral P. W. Brock wrote: 'Their assistance proved invaluable in the months that followed, not least in an unforeseen requirement that had arisen from the Potsdam Agreement, under which one-third of the battered ships of the Kriegsmarine (which had nearly all fetched up in our area) were to be repaired, stored and steamed to the Russian Zone with German crews.

'In the chaotic conditions still obtaining, their preparation was a major commitment. . .'

Members of the German Navy had to be retained for running the convoys of ships to Russian-held ports (known as the SCRAM convoys), to complete minesweeping off Kiel and similar duties. With the desperate conditions of the civilian population 'the presence of our Wrens, who played as hard as they worked, did much to keep the whole of Party 1734 civilised and cheerful.'

Admiral Brock was candid: 'I must admit that initially I feared that they might add to our security and transport problems, but their general popularity with all the Services ensured that escorts and cars were available on demand.'

Second Officer Diana Fletcher, who described herself as 'Senior Wren at Plon' wrote, when it was closing down: 'Other Wrens may have been further afield, seen more in the theatres of war or in warmer climes, but few can have felt more pride in their service or enjoyed more wonderful amenities than we of Naval Party 1734 at Plon.'

Wrens served in Minden, Hamburg, Wilhelmshaven, Cuxhaven, Bremen and Hanover, as well as Kiel, and in Berlin itself.

WRNS officers formed part of the staffs of the Prime Minister's overseas conferences with heads of state, notably in Quebec, Yalta and Tehran.

In December 1945 a party of twenty-four officers and nine ratings went from Sydney to Hong Kong for the headquarters of the British Pacific Fleet's Commander-in-Chief. They were mainly communications and clerical personnel.

12

TRAINING–AND RELEASE

THE PEAK NUMBER IN THE WRNS was reached in September 1944 when there were 74,635 officers and ratings, in 90 categories and 50 branches.

After that numbers fell and fluctuated gradually until releases under the Government's scheme began. Those of married officers and ratings in the high priority groups began in March 1945 – which greatly affected cooks, stewards, writers, stores and administrative personnel.

By July five categories were declared redundant, and a further 22 obsolescent, so that no recruits were put into them.

The release and reallocation scheme worked smoothly enough: dealing with the massive numbers involved meant that it was a major administrative triumph.

There was no question this time of a week's notice. Each woman was allotted a release number, based on such factors as the date her Service began. From widely published advertisements as well as from notices in her Unit, she knew when to expect her 'demob'.

She got a clothing grant and coupons, civilian ration book and identity card, gratuity (based on length of service), a discharge certificate (which could be used as a reference) and two months' paid leave between leaving her unit and finally the Service. This last was designed to give her time to find a job and money to keep her while doing so.

Many officers and ratings were, however, still needed – the Service might be greatly reduced in size, but it was not phased out altogether. Those who wished, volunteered for periods of extended service. Small numbers of women continued to be recruited on short term engagements.

With the end of the war in Europe the pressure of work at home lessened and educational and instructional activities of various types were arranged, including participation in special university short courses and symposia, lectures in establishments and preparation for examinations and technical and academic qualifications for civilian life.

In the New Year's Honours of 1945 Mrs Laughton Mathews had been made DBE. Between 1945 and 1946 work went ahead on the peace-time role of the WRNS, and she contributed much that was valuable and sensible to this. In November 1946 she retired.

It had been said of her in no less a place than the House of Commons (in 1943 by Mrs T. Cazalet Keir, MP): 'She combines two very important qualities in a leader, great humanity and sound common-sense. These qualities have assisted to build up complete harmony and confidence between Wrens of all ranks . . .'

Mr (afterwards Sir John) Lang, Acting Secretary of the Admiralty, wrote to her on November 25:

> 'I am commanded by My Lords Commissioners of the Admiralty to convey to you, on the occasion of your relief as Director of the WRNS, an expression of their high appreciation of the services which you have rendered during your tenure of that appointment.
>
> 'You were successful in bringing into the present Service the experience and traditions of the previous Corps. Throughout its development to its highest strength of 75,000 you were able to infuse into it the high standards of the Royal Navy and to avoid many of those difficulties apt to beset a new Service. The wide range of activities in which the WRNS has been employed is due largely to your inspiration and guidance.
>
> 'In your responsibility for the morale and well-being of the Service, you have won for the WRNS the trust and esteem of the public.
>
> 'My Lords are glad that you have been able to remain as Director . . . until the war-time purpose of the WRNS has been fulfilled and the process of transformation to the future organisation far advanced, so that the peace-time force will be built up on foundations laid by you.'

As Director she had found time to travel thousands of miles to visit Wrens, to cope with an immense workload at Headquarters, the illness and death of a much-loved husband, the evacuation and return of her growing family (her daughter, Elvira, became a Wren in 1943).

She was a remarkable woman in a remarkable job which she did remarkably well. Her own story of World War Two Wrens, *Blue Tapestry,* is warm-hearted, compulsive reading. Only she could have told it.

She was President of the Association of Wrens from 1952, presiding at post-war reunions, and introducing Prince Philip to that of 1957 with the often-quoted 'Girls — he's here!'

She enjoyed another career — this time in gas management — from 1947 until 1959. On her birthday that year (September 25) she died after a long illness.

One of her favourite speeches when visiting Wrens is worth repeating:

> 'Wrens, you are privileged to serve with the Royal Navy, the greatest Service in the world. Your work is tremendously important because behind it is something that may alter the face of the world and upon which all our ideals of living depend.
>
> 'Some of your jobs seem more glamorous than others but all are part of the pattern and are equally necessary — the only thing that matters is to do the job for which one is personally best fitted and to do it with all one's might.
>
> 'You have built up a Service of which the Navy is proud and that the country has confidence in. Do not forget that the reputation of that Service depends on every single one of you.
>
> 'Our lives are going to be wider and deeper because of all we have learnt in the Service. And when peace comes you will take your place in civilian life to such good purpose that people will say "Well, you see, she was a Wren".'

One of her great achievements was the training of officers and ratings. The Royal Naval College, Greenwich, was chosen for its tradition and atmosphere as the place to train officers. There the Officers' Training Course stayed — for a long time under Superintendent Elsie French — until bombing forced its move in April 1944 to Framewood Manor, Stoke Poges, Buckinghamshire. In December it returned to London, to New College, Hampstead, and in June 1945 to Greenwich.

It is an indication of the sound choice that it remained at

Greenwich until 1976, when fundamental Service changes dictated its move to Britannia Royal Naval College, Dartmouth, where training is alongside that of junior Naval officers.

The first organised general service training for ratings began in January 1940 at King's College, Campden Hill, Kensington. Here 90 trainees were housed, mainly those called up by Headquarters.

In June 1940 there was a move to the Queen Anne block at Greenwich (where the OTC was) which provided accommodation for 230 trainees. Towards the end of that year it was agreed that new entries would serve a fortnight's probation before enrolment and kitting-up, but the urgent demands from Commands meant that many women stayed, in fact, only two or three days.

Kitting-up was not always possible, for large quantities of WRNS clothing had been blitzed.

In March 1941 it was decided that no new entries should be entered in specific categories, but should come in as Probationary Wrens, and their futures should be decided in the Training Depot.

From 1941 the Chief Officer in charge of the Depot was also responsible for overseas drafts. Initially these were accommodated in the Depot, but as trainees increased in number so too did numbers awaiting transport overseas, and the latter went first to Golden Square, London, and later to Crosby Hall, Chelsea.

By April 1941 the expansion of the Service meant that there was no longer room for both officers' and ratings' training at Greenwich. Westfield College, Hampstead, was also used for ratings' training, and in June that year 730 ratings were under training at Greenwich and Hampstead.

There were Port Training Depots at Devonport, Chatham, Portsmouth, Liverpool and Rosyth, and attempts to introduce standardised training were prevented by limits of the available accommodation and the constant, urgent need for Wrens and yet more Wrens.

In March, 1942, New College, Hampstead was taken over for ratings' training, and thereafter no more were trained at Greenwich.

In that same month the National Service Acts for Women came into force. The Ministry of Labour would not allow National Service candidates to be put on a waiting list for entry. With this pressure, and the growing demands from Combined Operations bases for Wren personnel, the Central Training Depot at Mill Hill, London (capacity 900 trainees) was a timely acquisition.

In February, 1943, when the centralisation of general training was achieved, all mobile ratings were called there for their probationary period, except for a short spell in 1944 when flying bombs were at their worst.

Tulliechewan Castle, Balloch, was opened originally to take new entries from Scotland and the North, but, after a period of closure, re-opened just in time to take all new entries, while Mill Hill was considered unsafe. Joan Carpenter was in charge, until her move to Western Approaches, and thence to Headquarters as Deputy Director (Welfare). The Castle became Admiralty property in June 1943 and was finally released early in 1945.

Westfield was released in July, 1945, and Burghfield Camp, near Reading (formerly a Ministry of Supply camp) was taken over. Crosby Hall was soon released too, but Mill Hill continued to be the general service training depot until February, 1946. Then the Central Training Depot for all new entries was at Burghfield, where, now named HMS DAUNTLESS, it still is.

But in 1980 new entry WRNS ratings will be trained alongside RN ratings newly joined, at HMS RALEIGH, Torpoint, Cornwall, not far from Plymouth.

In the early days most people outside the WRNS considered training Wrens for particular jobs was unnecessary—'Let them pick up the job on the job'—and approved training for most categories which might be termed technical, had to be fought for.

Notable exceptions to the trial and error method were W/T special operators, and also coders.

Telephone switchboard training began in 1940, and was followed by that for teleprinter operators, wireless duties, visual signallers, writers, supply assistants, domestic categories, radio mechanics, M/T drivers, torpedo-women and Fleet Air Arm maintenance categories.

The first purely WRNS technical training establishment—HMS FLEDGLING at Mill Meece—was opened in 1943 for air mechanics.

'I don't think the modern Wren really knows about the sort of jobs that we had during the War,' said Dame Jocelyn Woollcombe. 'Our longest training was for radio mechanics, but the girls who serviced torpedoes and other armaments, and worked as shipwrights, carpenters and so on to turn-round the landing craft on D-Day plus deserve mention. Some of the air mechanics became "qualified to sign" that an aircraft engine was tested and in order.'

At Mill Meece each of the four air mechanic branches had its own training but all learnt the use of tools, basic fitting and repairing, and the theory and practice of their own special part of the aircraft.

One cannot leave training without mentioning just one of the several gifted women who were responsible for it—Superintendent Elsie French. Almost every WRNS officer of the Second World War passed through her hands, and when she died in 1963, Dame Jocelyn wrote: 'Smiling, friendly, witty, charming to look at and modest to a degree about her own capacity, she nevertheless possessed a most penetrating eye . . . Her assessments were brilliant, but very just, and her criticisms always constructive.'

The officers who were cadets under her were acutely aware that within a day or two she knew the name of every newly joined member of the course, and could put the name to the face. She appeared to know everything that was going on and everyone who was involved in it. All-knowing, all-seeing, wise, fair, at first terrifying, yet on closer acquaintance regarded affectionately, she was known (not to her face) as 'Aunt Elsie'.

For every woman who has served in the WRNS, the abiding memories are of her own 'parish'—her own part of it, whether she was where the action was or in a quiet area. She may have seen only a part of the whole War, but she came away from the Service feeling that this was the part that mattered. There were those who served in several places and those who served in one, there were those who went abroad and those who did not.

Very few of them were really aware that they were responsible for a profound change in women's place in society.

Where World War One opened the doors for women at work, World War Two swung them wide to a tremendous range of opportunities, there for the taking.

After the first War there was a reverting to some pre-1914 attitudes. Since 1945 the attitude to the woman who sought a career rather than marriage (or perhaps in addition to it) has altered. Having a full-time paid job has become usual for a woman. A woman living on her own in her own home has become socially acceptable. The pattern of social life has changed, so that a woman now plays a part of her own, and is not accepted solely as the adjunct of husband, father or brother.

That this has developed even further will be seen in relation to the permanent Service.

13

THE PERMANENT SERVICE

DAME JOCELYN WOOLLCOMBE succeeded Dame Vera as Director in November, 1946, and on February 1, 1949, the Service became a permanent part of the Royal Navy.

Although not subject to the Naval Discipline Act, the WRNS was a disciplined force serving under its own disciplinary code. It was regarded in all respects, other than this separate disciplinary code, as part of the Royal Navy itself.

The post-war period was crucial and it was due chiefly to the Director's wisdom that conditions of service were obtained which provided a career structure, with pay calculated as a proportion of that paid to the men of the Royal Navy (meaning that upward changes automatically applied also to the WRNS and did not have to be argued for each time) and pensions.

The opportunity was open to all those serving to transfer to the permanent Service, provided that they were within the required age limits and had a reasonable prospect of further service.

It was typical that the Director personally visited units to explain the plans so that officers and ratings could decide whether or not to re-engage.

How could women best be used in peace when there was no longer the call to take the place of men needed to fight at sea?

It was decided that 24 categories would be open to ratings—under technical, clerical, semi-clerical, supply, household, medical and miscellaneous headings. Air mechanics were still wanted, radio ratings to install, test and maintain aircraft radio equipment (with the chance to fly 'in the course of her duties'), radar plotters, telegraphists, range assessors (to assist in training Naval aircrews by assessing film records and explaining the results of air gunnery and bombing practices), meteorologists and cinema operators, able not only to use a projector but also to repair films.

The three categories of Writer, familiar to wartime Wrens, were still required — general, pay and shorthand, together with signals staff. Clothing, victualling and air stores (the issue of aircraft components and flying clothing) were needed, as were Quarters assistants, cooks, stewards and switchboard operators.

Those with a genuine interest in nursing could join as sick berth attendants, and others might become dental surgery attendants (although this was noted as a short-term category, with promotion to Leading Wren only).

The Education category provided opportunities for instructional duties in general subjects, handicrafts or domestic science. Welfare was a category for those with existing service who had reached Petty Officer rate and were over twenty-five.

Regulating ratings were to be concerned with the organisation and discipline of ratings. Motor transport drivers must be 'prepared to handle a light lorry and do running repairs'. (Had they forgotten that wartime Wrens drove three-tonners?)

It was stressed that ratings in all categories shared equal opportunities for promotion to officer, and that all officers, except a few with specialist qualifications, were chosen from serving ratings.

Officers were appointed for WRNS administrative duties, to look after WRNS Quarters, to serve as secretaries in Naval establishments, and to carry out technical duties such as air radio and meteorology.

Probationary training for ratings was extended to four weeks. They volunteered for four years, and were then given the chance, as ratings, to sign on for two further periods, each of four years, and finally for a period which would enable them to complete 22 years' service.

They then qualified for a pension and terminal grant. All ratings were mobile and liable for service 'wherever the Admiralty may require'.

In 1955 the only prospect of overseas service was in Malta apart from one or two Allied Headquarters in Europe. Twenty years later things had greatly improved in that respect — there were fifteen overseas places in which WRNS officers or ratings or both might serve.

Barbara Day (now Wilson) was a Leading Wren Writer (S) from 1946 to 1949 — she was at the RN Air Station, Dale, Pembrokeshire, and then in the Admiral's office at Chatham. She was lucky enough to be spoken to by the late Princess Marina, Duchess of Kent, during an inspection at Dale, and she remembers the revival of Navy Days at Chatham, and all the work that entailed.

From New Zealand she wrote: 'Those three years were very happy ones'. She recalled that a very young David Attenborough was serving at Dale when he took part in *While the Sun Shines* for which she did the scenery.

Kathlyn Strudwick joined in 1949: she had hoped for something to do with machinery or maintenance, but instead became a writer.

> 'Life during the first four weeks seemed very strange, covering such things as cabin inspections, learning to be five minutes ahead of scheduled lecture times, calling officers "Ma'am", not being adrift after having been out for the evening, and — most important — being on time for meals, otherwise there might not be anything left to eat!
>
> 'When the time came to start Part II training — which was designed to give you the knowledge to do the job you had chosen, in the Naval way — things began to fall into place.
>
> 'The time spent in training during this period varied — a radar plotter would need to spend more time at her Part II training establishment than, say, a cook or steward.
>
> 'If one failed the examination at the end of the course, depending on one's reason for failure one might get a second chance, but if it was through laziness or through not having absorbed enough, you either changed to a less demanding category or left the Service.'

She went to Whale Island, to Plymouth, to London, to Oslo. She remembered with pleasure the special duties such as providing a Royal guard of honour, selling programmes at a film premiere, marching to the Cenotaph for Remembrance Sunday, taking part in a tattoo at the White City, and parading to Chelsea Barracks on the Sunday before the Coronation of Queen Elizabeth II.

S. Berrecloth, who served from 1953 to 1957 said: 'Really on looking back life was so full that one simply does not know where to begin or what to leave out.'

She was a range assessor at RN air stations, and was able to enjoy her hobbies of flying, gliding and rifle shooting. An outstanding memory is meeting the Duke of Edinburgh at Lossiemouth in 1955; another is when the pilots at Lossiemouth went across to the Royal

Air Force station at Kinloss and painted in large letters on the parade ground "Come to Lossie Air Day" (and the consequences . . .).

Pamela Ford spent four years as a meteorologist from 1949 to 1953, taking her specialised training at Kete, Pembrokeshire, and then going on to Eglinton, Bramcote, and Culdrose: 'I was able to do a lot of flying and sailing, and made many friends, with whom I am still in touch after twenty years . . .'

While Rosemary Short was in for six years, first as a rating and then as a Quarters officer. She recalled a day at HMS DAEDALUS when the Wrens—in protest at the food they were getting—organised a 'demo'. They refused what was offered one lunch-time and went out to eat in the town. She said: 'Later, when I became a Quarters Officer, I always made sure I had a couple of Wrens to help me make out the menus!'

Ann Marston (née Buckley) is cast in the same mould as the wartime volunteers—she was ten when she first became interested in the Wrens and from the age of fourteen she knew that she would eventually join. 'I must have driven the Birmingham recruiting office and the people who did recruiting displays in department stores mad, as anything to do with the Navy and I was there. I visited careers conventions, recruiting stands anywhere, every recruiting office I came across.'

She entered at the age of 17½ (the earliest possible date), did her DAUNTLESS training and then on to RN Air Station, Culdrose, for meteorological observer training: 'Observation, theory, plotting, charts, codes, etc. This was very interesting but a bit confusing— clouds and weather not only have names but also a code . . .'

Thence to Yeovilton where during one night watch she recorded a temperature of 0°F. It took some 400 men with picks and shovels to clear the runways of ice and snow.

On another occasion a funnel cloud was seen over the airfield, a miniature whirlwind, which was duly photographed and aroused much interest. Another day she went to the meteorological centre at Bracknell where a Naval liaison officer took her on a tour and she made detailed notes of what she had seen. It was sad that her Wren career ended with a discharge on medical grounds.

Of her time as Director, Dame Jocelyn Woollcombe has written, especially for this history:

'My time as Director was entirely concerned with the conversion of the wartime "temporary" WRNS into the permanent Service.

'This meant in the first place, two years of inter-Service meetings, since it was obviously desirable that the three women's Services should have, as far as possible, similar conditions and offer parallel careers.

'One important difference was the refusal of the Board of Admiralty to put the WRNS under the Naval Discipline Act. This led to minor difficulties between the Services but nothing of real importance, and the unique status of the Wrens continued to be a source of pride to both the Navy and the WRNS.

'With some difficulty the principle was established that the women's pay should be a proportion of the men's and not calculated on an entirely different scale, related to the pay of women in other professions, such as nursing.

'This was important as it meant that changes in men's pay would be automatically applied to women, who might otherwise have had to argue out every change on their own account. At one point the Treasury proposed that all consideration of offering pensions to women in the Services should be postponed for five years.

'At the meeting called to resolve this impasse, I was, in fact, the only woman present, the other two Services being represented by senior male officers! Perhaps it was lucky I was there, for I cannot remember anyone else round the table feeling very strongly about it.

'Once the conditions to be offered in the permanent Service were settled it became my task to visit establishments to explain them so that people could decide whether they wished to re-engage.

'It amuses me to remember that the idea of pensions after 22 years service was at first greeted with incredulous laughter. No one, they thought, would stay so long.

'We now know that many have stayed and benefited.'

Dame Jocelyn Woollcombe was succeeded as Director by the first rating to achieve the highest rank in the Service—Mary Lloyd. She became Director at a vital moment.

The peacetime, permanent Service was in its early youth, and the leadership shown by the new Director was all-important for the new image which the women's Services would show to the world.

She had integrity, she knew the WRNS inside out, and she had great charm, which was useful when dealing with her male counterparts, and socially when she represented the Service on many different occasions and in many places.

She was Director from 1950 to 1954, was made DBE, had a WRNS quarters building named after her, and after retirement married. But she was overtaken by a progressive, crippling illness and in 1972 she died.

Dame Nancy Robertson was her successor, being Director from 1954-58: 'My main objective was to consolidate the permanent Service and to ensure that there was a worthwhile career open to ambitious and well-qualified girls.'

She considered that the scope of interesting jobs — which had largely disappeared by the end of the war — should be widened, and found NATO conferences useful for girls stationed in Malta who were frequently sent off to conferences in different parts of Europe. She added:

'We were able, with the help of the then Director of Naval Intelligence, to ease our way into embassies in Europe where young officers were appointed assistants to Naval attachés — Paris and Rome were the first such.

'On the whole the fifties were, I think, a period of marking time and settling in. There was so much to do in establishing permanent accommodation and, as usual, so little money.

'There was fun too, as when a Wren team competed in the Windsor Horse Show. The Wrens took their full part in all Service sporting activities.'

After her came Dame Elizabeth Hoyer Millar (1958-61) who recalls her time as Director as a time of withdrawals:

'It was a period of withdrawing from a lot of Naval bases, and therefore of Wren units, mostly from air stations. The problem was to find them billets in order to keep the strength going to what was the ceiling we were allowed, and below which would have been uneconomic.

'Overseas postings were down, and we longed for more, as recruiting propaganda. But there was hope. Singapore was not far off having a Wren unit, also Mauritius.

'One thing I remember well, was achieving a more advantageous structure for Second Officers, as at that time they could not get in enough time for pension, when retired through age, or non-promotion.'

It was during this period, on June 28, 1952, to be precise, that a lifeboat was launched — the AGUILA WREN, for the Aberystwyth station. She was given in memory of the draft lost in the torpedoing of SS AGUILA in 1941, being paid for with money raised from families, friends and members of the WRNS.

The idea was that of Canon and Mrs Ogle, parents of Second Officer C. M. Ogle, who had been in charge of the draft, with Mr Edward Benjamin, father of Chief Wren C. M. B. Benjamin, as co-trustee. When Canon Ogle died his place was taken by Mr Edward Bacon, brother of Chief Wren P. Bacon.

A hundred donors travelled to Wales for the launching, attended by Dame Vera Laughton Mathews, wearing her uniform for the occasion, when Mr Benjamin handed over the boat to the Royal National Lifeboat Institution. Dame Vera said:

'I knew every officer personally and the team was carefully chosen from volunteers. It would be impossible to picture a finer company — we sent our best.

'When the news of the tragedy came there was consternation, not only in the WRNS but in the Navy. We were not inured then to tragedy — later losses (and there were many) came as a less personal shock. These were the pioneers.

'And I think their death brought home to many for the first time the realisation that these young women were not joining up to wear a smart uniform or to have a good time, that they accepted willingly a share in the hardship, the responsibility and the perils of Service life.'

The boat was named by the eighty-year-old mother of Third Officer K. Miller. AGUILA'S master and another officer travelled from Liverpool between voyages, and a blind World War One ex-WRNS officer came from Belfast to remember her niece, Third Officer C. A. B. Joy.

In 1952, too, Dame Katharine Furse died. She had been desperately disappointed that she had not been called on during World War Two by the WRNS, or consulted. She was, however, still President of the Association of Wrens, which opened its doors to serving Wrens in 1942.

14

THE PATTERN CHANGES

THE SIXTIES AND SEVENTIES have seen the greatest advances yet — if advance is the right word — in 'women's liberation'.

After a period of consolidation and gradual integration into the Royal Navy, members of the WRNS are now in the position of being considered equally with male officers or ratings, as appropriate, for appointments and drafts — except to units or situations in which they might find themselves in combat.

What they have attained is qualified equality. They are considered, with suitable training, to be capable of holding any post in their category or branch (not much advance really on World War Two) — but they must not fight in battle. This is not a restriction imposed on Russian women — but do Wrens want this 'privilege' in fact?

A Ministry of Defence Study Group was set up in January, 1974, with WRNS representation at the highest level, to 'identify and re-define the role of the WRNS for the next ten years and beyond, examine the organisation, employment and structure of the Service, and make recommendations' in the light of the wider opportunities open to women, the needs of the Royal Navy and the constraints of the Defence Budget.

Miss Mary Talbot, who was Director from 1973-1976, said:

> 'Like the country, the WRNS was over-administered. WRNS officers were looking outward towards more Naval appointments and similar shore training to Naval officers, and the Wrens too wanted to have equal responsibility with the sailor.
>
> 'They were getting near equal pay. It was the right time for a change of direction.'

The recommendations of the Study Group fell neatly into four sections. The opening of new jobs to women, changes in training to enable them to do more demanding jobs, changes in structure and terms of service to encourage new patterns of work and longer service, and administrative changes aimed at greater integration with the Royal Navy.

While some of this is still in the future, much has already happened.

It reflects the thoughts of the majority of the Directors in this period. Dame Jean Davies (now Lancaster), Director from 1961-1964 said: 'In my view the whole period since the end of the war was a gradual process of bringing our Service into line with the Navy.'

In her time more units were set up abroad, while others closed as the Navy moved out. New quarters were built but some—like the Duchess of Kent Barracks at Portsmouth—were subsequently the victims of changed Service circumstances, and were sold.

Dame Jean said: 'Gradually combined messing was accepted in air stations and conditions for technical training were very often made similar to those for the same categories in the Navy.'

She valued the meetings of heads of the three women's Services, and the international conferences on the role of women in NATO Defence.

Dame Margaret Drummond (1964-1967) spoke for all the subsequent Directors, when she said: 'Policy planning in one era frequently does not take effect until the next, and similarly what is considered an achievement in one Directorship may be rescinded in another.'

Of her own time she said:

'All in all those years would probably be considered as a time of consolidation with good recruiting both for officers and ratings.

'The new units in Singapore and Mauritius were put on a sound basis and very good progress was made in bringing the accommodation in many units to peace-time standards.

'I had to appear before a Select Committee of the House of Commons to justify our remaining outside the jurisdiction of the Naval Discipline Act and I considered it to be of vital importance —with the Heads of Naval Personnel and Naval Law—that our status was upheld against considerable pressure to bring us into line with the other two women's Services.'

'The Naval Discipline Act' are four words which have been mentioned in WRNS circles since 1917. There have been strong arguments for and against the women's inclusion—it will be remembered that both Dame Katharine Furse and Dame Vera Laughton Mathews wanted the Service included but the then Boards of Admiralty would not hear of it.

Some of the post-War Directors have been in favour, others have not. With the anti-discrimination legislation, making it unlawful to use a person's sex as an objection to their holding a job, for example, there was a stronger argument *for* inclusion. Sex equality meant, surely, that the WRNS should be subject to the Act.

Miss Mary Talbot said: 'Although many are sorry to see us give up our unique status as the only Service not under a Discipline Act, it emphasises the change in our role — our determination to be equally trained and to take on more and more responsibilities within the Royal Navy.'

While it was announced in Miss Talbot's last year as Director that 'the WRNS be brought under the Act', this was not implemented until 1 July 1977 and was thus in the time of her successor, Miss S. V. A. McBride.

What makes a woman — without the stimulus of war or other national emergency — join the WRNS instead of going into a civilian job?

She accepts discipline, uniform, directions as to her work and where she does it, where she lives, and when she has her holidays. Only a few years ago this was for a salary much lower than that likely to have been earned as a civilian. Now, however, Service pay is more realistic.

Second Officer Vicky Hattersley was a private secretary in civilian life, and her Service appointments have included being personal secretary to the Second Sea Lord (at that time Admiral Sir David Williams). She said:

> 'In civilian life, if you change your job every two years or so, you get a reputation for being unreliable and changeable.
>
> 'In the Service it is the accepted practice to move every eighteen months to two years. So you get the change of surroundings, people and jobs because it is part of normal Service life.
>
> 'I think the WRNS offers me more prospects of senior employment than I could get as someone's secretary in business life.'

It is far from being all work in today's Wrens. Active, healthy people enjoy sport and the Navy has ever encouraged such activity. The WRNS does not lag behind.

There are young women going through the various stages towards the gold award in the Duke of Edinburgh's Award Scheme—already won by several Wrens. Others shoot, play tennis, golf, badminton or swim. Others take part in sponsored walks, or events such as the Ten Tors contest in the West Country.

This entails covering 35 miles over moorland terrain in 36 hours, including a 10-hour compulsory rest, cooking out of doors, pitching, sleeping in, and striking tents, and learning to live with others in an outdoor environment.

There is netball, sailing, amateur dramatics, and many other 'spare time' activities.

There have been many special occasions on which members of the Service have been privileged to take part—the Coronation of Queen Elizabeth II, the Investiture of the Prince of Wales, the funeral of Sir Winston Churchill, the tercentenary of the Royal Marines, the annual Royal Tournament.

Members of the Service are often included in the more adventurous Naval expeditions—for instance, two Leading Wrens went on an overland expedition to India—and one (possibly an officer) will almost certainly be on another trip, to the Lofoten Islands. A WRNS officer may be in an inter-Service yacht crew for one leg of a round-the-world yacht race.

There are still opportunities of overseas service, even though the Royal Navy is no longer maintaining bases in such well-known ports as Singapore (or even Malta). There are members of the WRNS in NATO Headquarters in Oslo, Naples, Lisbon and in Belgium, in Gibraltar, on exchange posts with the US Navy and the WRANS, and a small contingent is in Hong Kong.

There are occasional opportunities in exciting single posts: there is a Leading Wren in Peking in the Defence Attaché's office, one in New Delhi, one in Athens and another in New Zealand.

Travel of a different variety is offered in learning to ski, to canoe and to parachute.

There are 250 officers and 3,000 ratings in the modern Service and no shortfall of recruits. But in common with the Royal Navy, the WRNS faces a future that poses many unanswered questions.

Miss Talbot said: 'Since 1917 the shortage of manpower has always been the catalyst to opening up new opportunities for women . . .'

The future is as challenging as anything that has gone before. The present Director, Miss Vonla McBride, has said that it is to be hoped that, in resolving the questions and the problems, the WRNS does not lose its femininity nor yet its special relationship with the Navy.

As Dame Margaret Drummond has put it: 'Above all, I think the Service carries out its purpose of supporting the Royal Navy wherever and whenever required, while carrying on its tradition of very real concern for the individual officer and rating.'

15

THE FUTURE ROLE

by

THE DIRECTOR WRNS: COMMANDANT S. V. A. MCBRIDE, HON.ADC, BA

WHAT NEXT FOR THE WRNS? Ours is the last of the women's Naval services to integrate its administration with its parent Navy, and such integration must be handled with tact and care to be effective.

It is desperately important that integration does not mean a loss of femininity for the women, nor yet a competition with men for jobs within the Naval Service. Such is not why the women's Service exists — we are complementary, not supplementary.

How far can 'equality' go? Do women really want to be trained to fight? I think not. I think they may want to learn to fly Naval aircraft, they may want to serve at sea in a constructive and practical way, but not to bear arms in war. This is not a woman's way.

We must accept a certain limitation to the range of jobs available to us ashore, because there must be a satisfactory sea/shore employment ratio for the men of the Royal Navy.

Equality and integration have been the key words for some time now in employment, training and administration. Officers are filling posts ashore on the same terms as men, and WRNS ratings are judged and assessed for jobs on exactly the same basis as their male counterparts.

The training of officers has been aligned in that WRNS officers are now trained at Britannia Royal Naval College, Dartmouth, alongside the Royal Navy's junior officers. No longer are WRNS officer cadets trained at Greenwich for their future responsibilities.

From 1980 the training of Wren ratings will be at HMS RALEIGH, Torpoint, and not at HMS DAUNTLESS, Burghfield. The women will train alongside new entry Naval ratings, but at this early stage in their careers WRNS officers will continue to guide them through the impressionable, settling-in period. It is interesting to note that the US Navy, now much more fully integrated than we are, still considers it important that 'entry-level' training of women should be separate from that of the men.

Since January 1977 it has been the routine rather than the exception that WRNS officers and senior ratings should attend RN Divisional Courses. Places on the RN Staff Course and the Lieutenants' Greenwich Course are allocated to WRNS officers quite regularly, and they compete for the coveted psc (Passed Staff Course) notation on exactly the same terms as the men.

Regulating ratings of the WRNS are already being employed interchangeably with their Naval counterparts, WRNS Writers may soon be trained as full RN Writers, and serve with them on an equal basis. Welfare workers are being given the opportunity of obtaining professional civilian qualifications, which means a better and more professional service to families and individuals, and a WRNS PT category may be introduced very soon.

The Director of Naval Recruiting is responsible for recruiting Wrens as well as Naval ratings. The Flag Officer Admiralty Interview Board copes with WRNS officer selection as well as that of the Navy, while the Naval Secretary has taken over centralised RN and WRNS officer appointing. The Commodore Naval Drafting drafts both Naval and Wren ratings.

I, as Director, WRNS, am also Assistant Director General of Naval Personal Services, and WRNS personnel are well to the fore on all the staffs. There has been no take-over or even take-over bid for the WRNS. It is simply that we are accepted as 'just as good as' the Royal Navy. All other things being equal, a woman officer or rating can be considered for an appointment in the Naval Service just as well as a man.

I continue to advise the Admiralty Board on all matters affecting the WRNS and at Command level there is a senior WRNS officer who combines a 'naval' job with advising the Commander-in-Chief or Flag Officer.

RN and WRNS officers and senior ratings can now act as Divisional Officers for both RN and WRNS ratings — but all ratings may, if they so wish, see an officer of their own sex if they have a problem which they wish to discuss on a personal basis.

One of the most recent equalisers has been the decision that WRNS officers may also wear the same informal uniform as the men — the wool jerseys ('woolly pullies') with shoulder straps to indicate rank. Changes in the ratings' uniform are also contemplated.

Perhaps the biggest and most important change is that of bringing the WRNS under the Naval Discipline Act. This Act was reformed in 1971 and we are being brought into line with the other Women's Services in the country. But we shall still not commit Wrens to the detention cells. Perhaps one day we may decide to copy the MARVA of the Netherlands and get a deserter to pay the expenses of Naval police calling at her home, arresting her, and taking her into Naval custody. But not yet.

Whatever else the future holds it is certain that we shall be able to contribute our expertise in the knowledge that our professional and technical abilities will be recognised and used to the fullest extent possible.

We will have the great satisfaction of working within, rather than alongside, the Royal Navy.

16

HRH THE PRINCESS MARINA, DUCHESS OF KENT

1906-1968

ON THE OUTBREAK OF WAR the Duchess of Kent was appointed Commandant of the WRNS, a title which was to be changed to that of Chief Commandant. 'From the beginning she was determined to learn all about the Service; not least did she have to learn how to wear uniform correctly—in common with all the women who joined!' (Dame Jocelyn Woollcombe.)

Wherever she went during the War years—to air stations, to the home ports, to isolated small units—the sight of her was a tonic and her genuine, unfailing interest in what the Wrens were doing and how they lived was an inspiration.

She acted as a superb recruiter too. The morning after her broadcast in 1940, appealing for women to join the WRNS, the Recruiting Department at Headquarters was literally snowed under with applications. The staff begged that the Duchess should not be asked to do this again—she was too successful!

As the duties and categories of the Service expanded so she learnt more and more of what the Wrens did and where they served.

When the WRNS Benevolent Trust was launched she consented to be its President, and when the Association of Wrens opened its doors to the Wrens and ex-Wrens of World War Two, she became its Patron.

At the memorial service for her in Westminster Abbey on October 25, 1968, WRNS officers acted as ushers, and a contingent of members of the Service, together with the Director, were present, as were representatives of ex-Wrens, and the ex-Directors.

In a radio tribute on August 29 that year, Chief Officer Mary Talbot, then Deputy Director (and later to be Director), said:

'We in the WRNS feel her loss very deeply . . . because she was our own very special person. She wasn't just a figurehead who wore our uniform from time to time (and looked much better in it than anyone else).

'She was a friend and counsellor — always interested in the Wrens . . .

'During the war and after it her own courage was an inspiration to us. We genuinely appreciated her visits to our units and formalities were always cut to a minimum because she wanted to talk to and get to know as many Wrens as possible. The Wrens loved meeting her. Her ability to listen and be interested in them endeared her to everyone and Wrens were often less nervous or overcome with her than with many less important visitors.

'We were proud of her . . . and proud of her in our uniform — we never made any changes in it without referring to her first.

'We know that she took pride in being our Commandant, and that she had an affection for us, but she couldn't have known how great was our affection for her and how good her influence was upon us.

'She represented an ideal — which can be said of very few men or women in the world today.'

Members and former members of the Service have given in her memory garden seats in Kensington Gardens and at HMS DAUNTLESS.

H.M.S. WREN

A 'W' CLASS DESTROYER was named WREN, after the end of the 1914-18 War, and the Association of Wrens adopted her, presenting boat badges, a silk ensign and other items. This ship was lost off Harwich in 1940.

It was then officially suggested by the Second Sea Lord (Admiral Sir Charles Little) that the naming of another ship WREN would be an encouragement to the WRNS 'who were already giving' an excellent service'. . . . He further suggested that the Director should launch her.

With permission, members of the WRNS voluntarily subscribed some £4,000 towards the cost of building her, and the Director launched her at Messrs Denny's yard at Barrow-in-Furness in the summer of 1942.

She was a sloop and became one of the famous Second Escort Group under Captain F. J. (Johnny) Walker, sailing out of Liverpool.

It was ironic that in the 1950s she should be sold to the Germans.

In 1956 Chief Petty Officer James W. Bolton saw an advertisement offering WREN'S bell for sale at £15. He had been in her sick bay in 1953-55 when stationed in Bahrain, and had read the brass plate recording the gift of the sick bay's contents by relatives and friends of the WRNS draft lost aboard SS AGUILA.

He immediately telephoned Furse House, London, where Chief Wren Regulating Joan Turner advised him to contact Chief Officer S. Broster at the RN College, Greenwich, which he did. The latter got in touch with the Director of Stores and obtained the bell for HMS DAUNTLESS, and also the brass plate.

THE WOMEN'S ROYAL NAVAL RESERVE

THE WOMEN'S ROYAL NAVAL VOLUNTEER RESERVE was formed in 1952 — although London set up its nucleus unit in November 1951.

The officers and early senior ratings were almost all ex-WRNS while the junior ratings were all new to the Service.

They were attached to RNVR Divisions — Ulster, London, Severn, Tay, Forth, Clyde, Sussex, Humber, Mersey, Tyne and Solent — and on June 12, 1954, a representative contingent took part in the RNVR Jubilee Review on Horse Guards Parade.

From November 1, 1958, the word 'Volunteer' was dropped; the RNVR became the RNR and the WRNVR became the WRNR. By that date it was 11,000 strong.

The existing WRNR was composed of officers and ratings willing to be recalled in emergency to the WRNS and the title of this Reserve was changed to WRNSR at the same time.

Officers are required to do 14 days' continuous training per year; ratings (aged 18-40) without previous WRNS experience have 30 one-hour training periods in Part I Training, and then go on to follow the RNR training syllabus for their category to gain advancement. They are also obliged to train for 14 days continuously in a year.

Candidates aged 21-33 may be recommended for promotion to officer.

In the Reserve's 25th anniversary year there are 900 officers and ratings serving in eleven Divisions and six Units outside Divisions, and in eight RN Communications Centres.

THE ASSOCIATION OF WRENS

THERE ARE SIXTY BRANCHES in the British Isles and nine overseas. The Wren Association of Toronto and the Women's Royal New Zealand Ex-Service Women's Association (Inc) are affiliated.

It is possible to join the Association without joining a branch. Membership is open to any women who have served in the WRNS from 1917 to the present day, and to members of Queen Alexandra's Royal Naval Nursing Service and VADs who served with the Royal Navy.

Head office: 1A Chesham Street, London SW1X 8NL.

THE WRNS BENEVOLENT TRUST

The trust was started in 1941 and now assists about 220 people each year—women ranging in age from their twenties to their seventies and eighties.

Members of the WRNS who have served at any time after 3 September 1939 (unless deserters) and their dependants are eligible for assistance.

The kind of help given may vary from a regular allowance for an elderly ex-Wren to clothes for a young, deserted ex-Wren and her baby; from a grant to someone in great need of adequate home heating to the cost of installing or renting a telephone for a disabled ex-Wren.

Head office: 1A Chesham Street, London SW1X 8NL.

DAME VERA LAUGHTON MATHEWS AWARD

This is the Wrens' own memorial to the former Director, and provides a bursary for the daughter of an ex-Wren to study abroad in connection with her chosen career. A bursary may be awarded each year.

OTHER WOMEN'S NAVAL SERVICES

WOMEN'S NAVAL SERVICES, largely modelled on the WRNS, have been formed in Australia, Canada, New Zealand, South Africa, the United States of America, the Netherlands, Norway, Denmark, Turkey, in India and Free France during World War Two, and post-war in France.

Australia

The WRANS was formed in 1941 and disbanded at the end of the War. There were eventually some 3,000 of them and they served in all parts of the continent.

In 1951 it was decided to re-form the WRANS and Chief Officer Blair Bowden was appointed Director. When she left there were no WRANS officers with sufficient experience to take over and Chief Officer Joan Cole, WRNS, was seconded and appointed Director for two years.

Chief Officer E. Hill, WRNS, succeeded her in 1956, with headquarters in Melbourne, and 300 members of the WRANS to administer. During her time there she did 45,000 miles of air travel to visit units in Perth, Sydney, Canberra, Adelaide, Darwin, Brisbane and Hobart, Tasmania.

The women served as cooks, stewards, W/T operators, radar plotters, regulators, radio communications, writers, stores ratings and sick berth attendants.

In 1958 Chief Officer J. Streeter, WRANS (who had rejoined in 1954, having served in the War) became Director, remaining in office for twelve years. The present Director is Chief Officer B. D. McLeod, WRANS.

Canada

With the approval of the two Governments concerned, three WRNS officers went to start the WRCNS in 1942. They were Superintendent Joan Carpenter, Chief Officer (later Superintendent) Dorothy Isherwood (now Mrs Harvey Stubbs) and Second Officer Elizabeth Sturdee (now Lady Ashmore).

In three months they had to run a recruiting campaign, draw up conditions of service, agree categories, find a training centre and quarters, order uniforms and supplies, and attend numberless meetings on planning and organisation.

The first intake numbered 68 and a year later there were 3,000 members. Vast distances had to be covered in setting up and maintaining the Service. The ratings were trained at Galt, Ontario.

The Service is composed of volunteers, and is a part of the Royal Canadian Navy, subject to Queen's Regulations and Canadian Naval Orders.

The first Canadian woman to head the Service was Commander A. Sinclair, WRCNS.

New Zealand

The WRNZNS was approved in June 1942, and at first employed writers, cooks, stewards and W/T operators.

Women entered as probationary Wrens and were rated Wren after three months. The first commissioned rank was Fourth Officer, proceeding to Third, Second, First and Chief Officer.

The Service which has served with the RNZN since the war has now reached the point of integration.

South Africa

The SAWANS was formed in October 1943 and existed for war service only, being nicknamed the 'Swans'. They underwent a two-week disciplinary class at a South African Naval base, familiarising themselves with Naval customs, drill and the rudiments of a sailor's life and work.

This was followed by specialised training, except for those who entered for clerical duties, who were drafted after the initial fortnight. There were three branches—clerical, technical and communications.

'Swans' in the technical branch were called on to help man specialised Naval defence systems and had a thorough training, lasting up to four weeks, as well as having to pass a qualifying examination.

United States of America

The first 300 women reported for duty in the Navy Department, Washington, in December, 1942, and within two years there were 50,000 women serving, enlisted and sworn in. Originally called the Women's Reserve of the U.S. Naval Reserve (Waves) they are now totally integrated in the U.S. Navy, holding Naval ranks and rates (the Women's Armed Services Act was passed in 1948).

By 1946 WAVES held 44 ratings and a single one, that of seaman, involved women in 44 billets (akin to WRNS categories); while officers filled 102 billets (or branches).

Legislation authorising the service was signed in July, 1942, Mildred McAfee (later Horton) was the first Director, officers' advance training began in August (at Northampton, Massachusetts) while the first three enlisted schools opened in October. The first trained women reported for duty in November.

There were 10,000 women in the U.S. Naval Reserve as Yeomen (F) in 1918. One of them was Joy Bright, later Hancock, and from 1946-1953 Assistant Chief of Naval Personnel for Women (she rejoined in 1942).

The 1918 uniform was reminiscent of Nelson's sailors' round hats, worn with navy suits and white blouses, with the large collars worn outside the jackets.

In World War Two it was similar to that of the WRNS, but shortly afterwards it was re-designed and has since hardly altered. Officers and ratings have similar blue uniforms with distinguishing badges, simple grey working dresses for summer use, and white summer dress uniforms.

For further reading: *Lady in the Navy* by Joy Bright Hancock (The Naval Institute Press, Annapolis, 1972).

The Netherlands

The women's service of the Royal Netherlands Navy was formed in London in 1944 after the first officers had been trained by the WRNS. The MARVA badge includes the City of London's coat of arms to mark this. The MARVA rapidly became established and respected. Badges of rank were blue but now that the women are an integrated part of the RNN are red — as for the men. There have been close contacts always with the WRNS, including visits, exchanges and participation in training. Their motto is *Semper adjutans* (Always helpful)—'the Netherlands Wren is always ready for any duty she may be called upon to perform.'

Denmark

The Danish Women's Navy Corps is based on the WRNS, and was formed in June, 1946, after its first Director, Mrs M. A. von Lowzow, had studied the Wrens in England that April.

They were part of the Home Guard Associations now replaced by the Home Guard (a trained reserve which can be immediately mobilised in war) and have the same rights as the men in matters of law, pay, etc.

The uniform is modelled on that of the WRNS (the officers' hats come from the same maker) but ratings wear berets.

Norway

Women have, since the end of World War Two, volunteered to train with the Royal Norwegian Navy as reservists, for service in war.

From 1977 they will also be able to serve as fully integrated military personnel in the Navy, on three-year contracts. They will be volunteers and cannot serve in combat units or enter operational or engineering branches. There will be special six-month courses to fit women to be instructors and duty officers at Naval establishments where women personnel will be trained.

Reservists will continue, training largely in signals and operational trades, but now learning also to handle weapons, and will be called up for duty during peacetime exercises.

The uniform is being re-designed.

France

The Services Feminins de la Flotte were formed in Algiers among the Free French in 1940, and reached a maximum of 2,800. They virtually ceased in 1945–46 although a small group were in Indo-China until 1955.

In 1951 the Personnel Feminin de l'Armee de Mer were constituted, with direct entry officers of high academic level, and non-commissioned officers with professional qualifications for certain categories, such as secretarial.

In 1971 the Women's Services were expanded, and the PFAM had ratings equivalent to Wrens and Leading Wrens in addition to the existing levels of Service. It grew from 200 in 1971 to 600 in 1976.

In 1977 it was integrated with the French Navy. Officers had the option of returning to civilian life if they wished.

Future officers will come from those already serving, and women will be able to join direct from university with a degree qualification.

Belgium

A Women's Naval Service has been formed within the last year, and so far consists only of ratings, one of whom is attached to NATO. It is a part of the Royal Belgian Navy and its officers will probably be drawn from suitable ratings.

HONOURS

CBE (Mil)
Mrs M. L. Cane, Asst Director
Mrs W. Dakyns, MBE, Asst Director

Miss D. C. Hare, MD, Asst Director (Medical)

OBE (Mil)
Miss H. M. Beale, Dep Div Director
Miss C. E. Bennett, Dep Div Director
Miss M. I. Currey, Asst Director
Miss I. M. Jermyn, Div Director
Mrs W. M. de L'Hôpital, Dep Asst Director
Miss A. B. Maclennan, Dep Div Director
Miss E. I. F. Matheson, MBE, Div Director
Miss E. G. Merston, Dep Asst Director

Miss M. M. Monkhouse, Asst Director
The Hon Mrs E. M. Northcote, Div Director
Miss K. St A. Penrose, Div Director
Miss E. M. Royden, Dep Asst Director
Mrs B. Valpy, Dep Asst Director
Miss S. J. Warner, Dep Asst Director
Miss F. E. Warton, Dep Div Director

MBE (Mil)
Miss E. Best, Asst Principal
Miss F. E. Bradshaw, Asst Principal
Miss B. M. Craster, Principal
Miss A. I. Crisp, Dep Principal
Mrs D. S. M. Eastwood, Principal
Miss M. G. M. Farrell, Asst Principal
Miss O. H. Franklin, Dep Principal
Miss M. Godding, Asst Principal
Miss I. A. Gye, Dep Principal
Miss M. Hardie, Asst Principal
Mrs I. N. Horsey, Asst Principal
Miss E. M. James, Dep Principal
Miss K. M. James, Dep Principal
Miss E. G. Johnston, Asst Principal
Mrs F. Johnston, Dep Principal
Miss W. E. Kersey, Asst Principal

Miss E. S. M. Laughton, Principal
Miss M. L. MacDonald, Dep Principal
Miss O. M. Macleod, Asst Principal
Miss J. M. McEwan, Dep Principal
Miss B. N. Mouat, Asst Principal
Miss M. H. M. Maunsell, Asst Principal
Mrs I. H. C. Pettit, Dep Principal
Miss N. G. Robinson, Dep Principal
Miss I. M. Rope, Dep Principal
Mrs V. R. Rubenstein, Dep Principal
Miss M. C. E. C. Strickland, Asst Principal
Miss M. A. Thorburn, Asst Principal
Miss H. O. Turnbull, Asst Principal
Miss M. A. M. Wall, Principal
Miss G. M. Watts, Dep Principal

Medal of the BEO (Mil)
Miss E. B. Bell, CSL (Mech)
Miss M. Carter, CSL
Miss E. F. Coleman, Snr Wtr
Mrs K. Cummings, Sh Typist
Miss M. D'Arcy, CSL (Clerk)
Miss G. O. Dart, CSL (Draughtswoman)
Miss A. M. Davies, CSL (Clerk)
Miss A. S. Dennis, Clerk
Miss A. E. Dove, Motor Dvr
Miss D. Dove, CSL (Sh Typist)
Miss M. Duckworth, Sh Typist

Miss K. Duncan, Snr Wtr
Mrs M. F. Evans, CSL (Clerk)
Miss D. E. French, Snr Wtr
Miss R. Hayter, CSL (Steward)
Miss H. F. Henderson, Tel Op
Miss A. H. Jenner, Motor Dvr
Miss M. E. S. E. Maunsell, CSL (Elec)
Miss E. O. Perrett, SL (Steward)
Mrs A. A. Reid, Snr Wtr
Miss J. Smith, CSL
Miss I. G. Tidman, CSL (Sh Typist)

BEM   **1940**
Ldg Wren N. Marsh

BEM   **1941**
Wren P. B. McGeorge

CBE   **1942**
Mrs E. S. M. Laughton Mathews, MBE, Director

MBE
Miss M. E. P. Pelloe, 2/0   Miss P. I. N. Grace, 3/0

BEM
Ch Wren M. W. Hastings   P/O E. M. Reid

CBE   **1943**
Miss E. M. Goodenough, Dep Director   Miss J. Carpenter, Supt

OBE
Mrs E. M. Mackenzie-Grieve, ex-Supt   Miss E. M. French, Ch Offr

MBE
Mrs M. R. Rathbone, A/1/0   Miss J. Madge, 2/0
Mrs C. H. Finch-Noyes, 2/0   Miss J. M. Shakespear, 2/0
Miss N. K. Kellard, 2/0   Miss R. S. Redmayne, A/2/0

BEM
Ch Wren E. Alford   P/O B. M. Rooke
Ch Wren H. L. Bareham   P/O M. H. Smith
Ch Wren E. F. Toogood   Miss C. H. D. Duff, 3/0 (as Wren)
P/O K. V. Harris

CBE   **1944**
Mrs E. V. Welby, Supt   Miss J. M. Woollcombe, Supt

OBE
Miss E. F. Stubbs, Ch Offr

MBE
Mrs G. O. Snow, Ch Offr   Miss F. P. Chase, 2/0
Miss F. Potter, A/Ch Offr   Miss B. M. B. Drabble, 2/0
Miss J. Davies, 1/0   Miss A. M. Whittaker, 2/0
Miss H. Hayes, 1/0   Miss D. V. Chaworth-Musters, 3/0
Miss L. E. Medley, 1/0   Miss N. D. May, 3/0
Miss H. E. Archdale, 2/0   Miss J. M. F. Sopper, 3/0

BEM
Ch Wren M. E. Dasnieres   P/O A. Knowles
Ch Wren K. M. Kimber   P/O A. L. Leithead
Ch Wren M. B. Matches   P/O A. Moyes
Ch Wren R. K. Stratford   P/O E. M. Pargeter
Ch Wren C. E. Vaughan   Ldg Wren A. A. Paton
P/O H. Cameron   Wren E. G. Booth

DBE   **1945**   **CBE**
Mrs E. S. M. Laughton Mathews, CBE,   Miss A. J. Currie, Supt
  Director

OBE
Miss M. G. Bois, Ch Offr   Miss J. T. Kidd, Ch Offr

MBE
Miss E. Eldod, 1/0
Mrs J. M. B. Elliot, 1/0
Mrs M. I. Thomas, 1/0
Mrs J. M. Wiles, 1/0
Miss E. M. Candy, 2/0

Mrs N. M. Conner, 2/0
Miss H. M. Minto, 2/0
Miss E. Shuter, 2/0
Miss B. M. Towle, 2/0

Chevalier (Belgium)
Miss M. K. Luckham, Ch Offr
Miss E. M. Harbord, 1/0

Miss M. F. K. Whitehouse, 2/0

BEM
Ch Wren G. G. Boulton
Ch Wren B. M. Browne
Ch Wren J. G. Bryan
Ch Wren H. L. Cheshire
Ch Wren F. Crowther
Ch Wren E. P. Gould
Ch Wren M. F. Halton
Ch Wren L. M. Hooper
Ch Wren O. King
Ch Wren P. C. Mather
Ch Wren N. E. M. Mitchell
Ch Wren B. C. Moyes
Ch Wren Y. E. Powell
Ch Wren E. M. Ross
Ch Wren B. Watson
Ch Wren T. L. Yorke
P/O M. Beckley
P/O R. V. L. Brown
P/O N. E. Gallagher

P/O C. E. Hart
P/O K. S Holmes
P/O M. E. Howes
P/O E. D. Land
P/O J. E. Pearce
P/O M. Raithby
P/O P. M. L. Schoon
P/O D. A. Shipley
P/O F. Suffield
P/O M. A. Toland
P/O K. White
Ldg Wren D. E. Batchelor
Ldg Wren J. V. Blundell
Ldg Wren J. Catchpole
Ldg Wren A. Cross
Ldg Wren P. A. Hannington
Ldg Wren I. J. London
Ldg Wren J. H. Prior
Wren P. M. Thomas

Croix de Guerre (Belgium)
P/O J. B. Carle
P/O W. C. Godden

P/O A. B. Munro

CBE   1946
Mrs G. L. Bell, Supt
Mrs V. C. S. Boyd, Supt

Miss A. Curtis, MBE, Supt
The Marchioness of Cholmondeley, Supt

OBE
Miss M. K. Lloyd, Supt
Miss M. I. Cooper, Ch Offr
Miss H. R. Herrick, Ch Offr
Miss D. A. Hesslegrave, Ch Offr
Miss A. McNeil, Ch Offr

Miss P. D. Nye, Ch Offr
Mrs A. F. Parker, Ch Offr
Miss N. M. Robertson, Ch Offr
Miss B. Samuel, Ch Offr
Miss S. M. Stuart-Thompson, Ch Offr

MBE
Miss H. L. Overy, Ch Offr
Miss J. M. Stewart, A/Ch Offr
Miss T. Ziman, A/Ch Offr
Miss G. M. Ballantyne, 1/0
Miss M. M. Bray, 1/0
Miss M. E. Buckland, 1/0
Miss J. M. Brunton, 1/0
Miss E. I. Collier, 1/0
Mrs K. M. A. Earnshaw, 1/0
Miss P. M. Frankland, 1/0
Miss E. W. Gibson, 1/0
Miss M. E. Keen, 1/0

Miss M. H. Love, 1/0
Miss P. L. Murray, 1/0
Miss D. K. Russell, 1/0
Miss P. Somers-Brown, 1/0
Miss J. K. Taylor, 1/0
Mrs C. M. R. Wood, 1/0
Miss N. E. Bond, 2/0
Miss V. E. B. Cannon, 2/0
Miss M. L. Carter, 2/0
Miss P. J. Cookman-Roberts, 2/0
Miss Y. S. Curtis, 2/0
Miss G. A. Gibson, 2/0

Miss E. S. Grain, 2/0
Miss B. J. Grylls, 2/0
Miss A. R. Haldin, 2/0
Miss L. E. G. Howe, 2/0
Miss M. S. Howie, 2/0

Miss M. O. Liddell, 2/0
Mrs M. Naish, 2/0
Mrs A. D. Niven, 2/0
Miss F. J. Porteous, 2/0
Miss A. L. Simonds, 3/0

Legion of Merit (France)
Mrs N. D. Coward, MBE, 2/0

Bronze Star Medal
Miss E. G. Trubody, 1/0

BEM
Ch Wren E. D. D. M. Banks
Ch Wren B. M. Buck
Ch Wren M. W. Clarke
Ch Wren M. Clough-Ormiston
Ch Wren B. E. E. Coe
Ch Wren R. E. Cooper
Ch Wren A. Cox
Ch Wren N. L. Craig
Ch Wren D. Farmer
Ch Wren L. M. Ferguson
Ch Wren E. I. J. Hall
Ch Wren E. M. Hammond
Ch Wren A. A. C. Hiles
Ch Wren M. E. Jones (*Jan*)
Ch Wren M. E. Jones (*June*)
Ch Wren E. M. Loynes
Ch Wren B. McDonald
Ch Wren D. M. Murphy
Ch Wren K. P. O'Kane
Ch Wren A. B. L. Sampson
Ch Wren E. Shannon
Ch Wren E. L. Skinner
Ch Wren E. J. Smith
Ch Wren M. M. Smith
Ch Wren A. M. Stutter
Ch Wren A. W. Thomson
Ch Wren D. I. M. Tucker
Ch Wren O. Wheeler
Ch Wren M. Wild
Ch Wren E. H. Wilkinson
P/O O. A. Adlington
P/O J. M. Andrews

P/O J. B. Carle
P/O D. Dewhurst
P/O J. A. Foster
P/O W. C. Godden
P/O J. Heeley
P/O M. J. Herbert
P/O M. C. Hilson
P/O W. M. Hopkins
P/O M. E. Hyslop
P/O M. M. McMeecham
P/O M. E. W. Marle
P/O V. E. Ollerenshaw
P/O H. Phillis
P/O J. P. M. Skidmore
P/O J. Thomas
P/O M. Whitney
A/P/O M. A. T. L. Blesse
Ldg Wren T. Beere
Ldg Wren E. M. Harbour
Ldg Wren M. E. Nyland
Ldg Wren E. A. Sparks
Ldg Wren J. Steinfeld
Ldg Wren M. R. Stewart
Ldg Wren P. D. Stuart
Ldg Wren E. Watson
Ldg Wren J. B. Wheeler
Ldg Wren L. A. Wiley
Wren E. J. E. Aitkenhead
Wren I. M. Bellamy
Wren E. G. Brain
Wren E. E. G. Grant
Wren J. A. Higgins

Bronze Star Medal
P/O E. M. Briscoe

CBE 1947
Miss D. Isherwood, Supt

OBE
Miss J. Frith, Supt
Mrs M. F. Miller, Supt

MBE
Miss R. Sheepshanks, 1/0
Miss J. Foster, A/3/0

BEM
Ch Wren J. Mackenzie Barr
Ch Wren K. Thompson
Ch Wren E. M. Walsh

P/O M. L. Bowman
P/O M. Dickinson
P/O E. M. Driscoll

Order of Orange Nassau (Netherlands)
Dame V. Laughton Mathews, DBE, Director, Grand Officer

Mrs N. Swayne, Ch Offr — Officer
Miss C. Eyton, 1/0 — Officer

Haakon VII Liberty Medal (Norway)
Ch Wren Y. E. Powell

Ldg Wren H. L. M. Banfield

Indian Independence Medal
Miss J. Foster, A/3/0

CBE 1948
Miss M. B. Rundle, Supt

MBE
Miss C. Fletcher, 1/0

BEM
Ch Wren E. L. Southern
P/O M. L. Hubbard

P/O P. E. Neale

OBE 1949
Mrs B. F. M. Lacey, Ch Offr

MBE
Miss F. M. Ingledew, 2/0

BEM
Ch Wren K. C. Dickinson
Ch Wren C. G. M. Morgan

Ch Wren E. Parke
Ch Wren D. K. Southey

DBE 1950
Miss J. M. Woollcombe, CBE

CBE
Miss A. McNeil, OBE

MBE
Miss M. L. Campbell, 2/0

BEM
Ch Wren P. E. M. Sanders
P/O M. A. Day

P/O G. Jones

MBE 1951
Miss J. M. Hales, 2/0

BEM
Ch Wren P. G. Heard
Ch Wren J. N. Logan

Ch Wren E. A. Morfey
Ch Wren J. Ramsay

DBE 1952
Miss M. K. Lloyd, OBE, Commdt

OBE
Miss E. L. E. Hoyer-Millar, Supt

MBE
Miss E. S. Colquhoun, 2/0

BEM
Ch Wren B. W. Barron
Ch Wren A. McNabb

Ch Wren R. M. Morton
Ch Wren S. M. Piper

CBE 1953
Miss N. M. Robertson, OBE, Supt

MBE
Mrs D. E. Hollinghurst, 1/0

BEM
Ch Wren J. L. Maltman
Ch Wren V. Martin
Ch Wren J. B. Owen

P/O N. Crawford
P/O I. J. Jeffery

OBE 1954
Miss E. M. Hampson, Ch Offr

MBE
Miss I. M. Austen, 2/0   Miss L. M. Ridley, 2/0

BEM
Ch Wren A. E. M. Hawkins   Ch Wren M. McColgan
Ch Wren E. M. Jenkyn

OBE 1955
Miss C. A. Lawson, Ch Offr

BEM
Ch Wren G. M. Brown   Ch Wren M. I. McLachlan
Ch Wren I. E. David   Ch Wren L. Roper

MBE 1956
Miss B. M. Hooppell, 1/0

BEM
Ch Wren R. C. A. Dalley   Ch Wren J. E. McManus

DBE 1957
Miss N. Robertson, CBE, Commandant

OBE   **MBE**
Mrs S. H. Broster, Ch Offr   Miss M. L. Doughty, 1/0

BEM
Ch Wren B. E. Chapman   Ch Wren J. L. Turner

OBE 1958
Miss J. Davies, Ch Offr

MBE
Miss I. K. Steljes, 1/0   Miss D. M. Noakes, A/2/0

BEM
Ch Wren W. Robinson   A/Ch Wren S. Bainbridge

OBE 1959
Miss M. A. P. Cook, Supt   Miss W. J. Denham, Ch Offr

BEM
Ch Wren E. I. Boyd   Ch Wren E. E. Garbutt
Ch Wren G. H. M. England

ARRC
P/O (SB) K. E. A. Funnell

DBE 1960
Miss E. L. E. Hoyer-Millar, OBE, Commandant

OBE   **MBE**
Miss E. M. Drummond, Ch Offr   Miss I. J. Scott, 1/0

BEM
Ch Wren M. V. Penney   Ldg Wren S. J. V. Craven

BEM 1961
Ch Wren I. Atkinson
Ch Wren V. Keys

Ch Wren V. L. Pollard

OBE 1962
Miss E. G. Lucas, Ch Offr

MBE
Miss P. Cooper, 1/0

BEM
Ch Wren A. Chasty
Ch Wren D. Holland

Ch Wren K. V. A. Moth
Ch Wren V. M. Perrin

DBE 1963
Miss J. Davies, OBE, Superintendent

OBE
Miss J. Cole, Ch Offr

MBE
Miss J. M. de Glanville, 1/0

BEM
Ch Wren I. Morton
Ch Wren P. M. Oxer

Ch Wren E. M. Reardon

CBE 1964
Miss M. M. Kettlewell, Superintendent

BEM
Ch Wren M. C. Macmillan

P/O G. D. Hinde

BEM 1965
Ch Wren G. A. Barnes

Ch Wren D. E. Philipson

DBE 1966
Miss E. M. Drummond, OBE, Commandant

CBE
Miss B. S. Brown, Supt

OBE
Miss M. R. Bammant, Ch Offr

BEM
Ch Wren B. Ellwood

Ch Wren R. A. Gallagher

BEM 1967
Ch Wren A. E. R. Murrell

Ch Wren J. M. Smith

BEM 1968
Ch Wren E. M. Husted

Ch Wren E. J. Young

OBE 1969
Miss J. S. Rae, Ch Offr (Died before receiving award)

MBE
Miss S. G. Pert, 1/0

BEM
Ch Wren B. J. Jones
Ch Wren E. M. Howard

DBE 1970
Miss M. M. Kettlewell, CBE, Commandant

MBE
Miss D. Graham, 1/0

BEM
Ch Wren M. F. Fenton
Ch Wren I. Holmes

Ch Wren M. See

BEM   **1971**
Ch Wren M. L. Clarke   Ch Wren V. M. Parry

CB   **1972**
Miss D. M. Blundell, Commandant

OBE   **BEM**
Miss N. A. Swainson, Ch Offr   Ch Wren J. K. Hall

BEM   **1973**
Ch Wren B. Young

CBE   **1974**
Miss J. Cole, OBE, Superintendent

BEM
Ch Wren M. B. Cridge   Ch Wren I. M. Knight
Ch Wren J. G. Fraser

CB   **1975**
Miss M. I. Talbot, Commandant

BEM
Ch Wren P. Read

MBE   **1976**
Fleet Chief D. M. Gordon   Fleet Chief J. F. King

WOMEN'S ROYAL NAVAL RESERVE

MBE   **1967**   **BEM**
Miss K. Stewart, 2/0   Wren R. Tattersall

BEM   **1971**
Ch Wren J. N. Rogers   Wren J. P. Searle

BEM   **1972**
Ch Wren M. Pacheco

MBE   **1975**   **BEM**
Miss M. E. Morse, Ch Offr   Ch Wren G. A. E. Coulson

BEM   **1976**
Ch Wren V. B. Dyson

BIBLIOGRAPHY

Never at Sea	edited V. Laughton	Private 1919
Hearts and Pomegranates	Dame Katharine Furse	Peter Davies 1940
Blue Tapestry	Dame Vera Laughton Mathews	Hollis & Carter 1948
Never at Sea	Commandant V. McBride	Educational Explorers 1966
The Punch Book of Women's Rights	Constance Rover	Hutchinson 1967
The Navy at War 1939-45	Captain S. W. Roskill	Collins 1960
Victory at Sea	Lt Cdr P. K. Kemp	Muller 1958
How We Lived Then	Norman Longmate	Hutchinson 1971
Blue for a Girl	John Drummond	W. H. Allen 1960
The Story of the WRNS	Eileen Bigland	Nicholson & Watson 1946
c/o GPO London	Rosemary Curtis-Willson	Hutchinson 1949
The Inner Circle	Joan Bright Astley	Hutchinson 1971
Suffragettes International	Trevor Lloyd	BPC Unity 75 1971
Max Horton & the Western Approaches	Rear Adml. W. S. Chalmers	Hodder & Stoughton 1954
Modern Britain 1885-1955	Henry Pelling	Cardinal 1969
One Marine's Tale	Gen. Sir Leslie Hollis	Deutsch 1956
Women	Katharine Moore	Batsford 1970
Daughters of Britain	V. Douie	Douie, Oxford 1946
Anglaises en Uniform	P. Dupays	Editions de la Critique Paris 1951
Women at War	M. Goldsmith	Lindsay Drummond 1943
They Made Invasion Possible	P. Scott	Hutchinson 1944
Women in Uniform	D. Wadge Collett	Sampson, Low Marston 1946
Wrens in Camera	Lee Miller	Hollis & Carter 1945
The World at War	Mark Arnold-Foster	Fontana/ Collins 1976
Scapa Flow	M. Brown and P. Meehan	Allen Lane 1968
Services Wrendered	Captain J. Broome	Kimber 1974
Service Women	Chief Officer V. Reynolds	Educational Explorers 1977

INDEX